Preface

to the *Essays* of Michel de Montaigne
by his Adoptive Daughter,
Marie le Jars de Gournay

MEDIEVAL & RENAISSANCE TEXTS & STUDIES

VOLUME 193

Preface

to the *Essays* of Michel de Montaigne
by his Adoptive Daughter,
Marie le Jars de Gournay

Translated, with Supplementary Annotation, by

Richard Hillman & Colette Quesnel

from the edition prepared by François Rigolot

MEDIEVAL & RENAISSANCE TEXTS & STUDIES
Tempe, Arizona
1998

© Copyright 1998

Arizona Board of Regents for Arizona State University

Library of Congress Cataloging-in-Publication Data

Gournay, Marie Le Jars de, 1565–1645.
    Preface to the Essays of Michel de Montaigne by his adoptive daughter, Marie Le Jars de Gournay / translated, with supplementary annotation, by Richard Hillman & Colette Quesnel from the edition prepared by François Rigolot
      p. cm. — (Medieval & Renaissance texts & studies ; v. 193)
    Text in French with English translation on opposite pages; introd. and notes in English.
    Includes bibliographical references.
    ISBN 0-86698-235-3 (alk. paper)
    1. Montaigne, Michel de, 1533–1592. Essais. 2. Gournay, Marie Le Jars de, 1565–1645. I. Hillman, Richard, 1949– . II. Quesnel, Colette. III. Rigolot, François. IV. Title. V. Series.
PQ1643.G63 1998
844'.3—dc21   98-8719
                                                                                            CIP

This book is made to last.
It is set in Garamond,
smythe-sewn and printed on acid-free paper
to library specifications.

Printed in the United States of America

Table of Contents

Acknowledgments	vii
Introduction, by Richard Hillman	1
Translators' Explanatory Note	19
Marie de Gournay, Préface á l'édition des *Essais* de Montaigne (1595), edited by François Rigolot	20
Marie de Gournay, Preface to Montaigne's *Essays* (1595), translated by Richard Hillman and Colette Quesnel	21
Works Cited	105

Acknowledgments

The translators wish to express their gratitude to Philippe Desan, editor of *Montaigne Studies: An Interdisciplinary Forum*, for granting permission to reprint Marie de Gournay's "Préface à l'édition des *Essais* de Montaigne (Paris: Abel L'Angelier, 1595)" in the edition by François Rigolot, which originally appeared in that journal (vol. 1, November 1989). Our project has also been aided financially by The University of Western Ontario, thanks to J. M. Good, Dean of Arts, and by the research and technical assistance of Cecily Devereux (now of The University of Alberta). Joseph Black, formerly curator of the Centre for Reformation and Renaissance Studies, Victoria University in the University of Toronto, was especially obliging in meeting our research needs, as was the staff of the Fisher Rare Book Library, University of Toronto. David Galbraith (The University of Toronto) did us a timely bibliographical favor. Encouragement for the project at an early stage was provided by François Paré (The University of Guelph) and Donald Beecher (Carleton University); in the latter stages, we have benefitted greatly from the interest and advice of Robert E. Bjork, Director of Medieval & Renaissance Texts & Studies.

Our foremost scholarly and personal debt is to François Rigolot (Meredith Howland Pyne Professor of French Literature, Princeton University), who has been unfailingly generous in his practical and moral support over several years—support that merely began with agreement to allow his edition, including annotations, to be used as a basis for our translation. Thereafter, his openness to consultation and to the evolving nature of the project effectively involved him in our own sustained collaboration.

Introduction

In offering the first English translation of Marie de Gournay's "Preface" to her initial edition of Montaigne's *Essais* (1595), Colette Quesnel and I aim at redressing for Anglophone readers the same deficiency to which François Rigolot was responding when, in 1989, he produced the first French edition of the 1595 Preface since its original appearance.[1] The multiple editions of the *Essais* over a forty-year period (from 1595 to 1635) following their author's death reflected the tireless promotion and the assiduous editorial labors of Marie de Gournay, Montaigne's "fille d'alliance" [adoptive daughter]. Yet from the time of Marie de Gournay's own death in 1645 (at the age of 79), the celebrated masterpiece of her "father" was virtually severed from her name. Post-seventeenth-century editions of the *Essais* do not include any of the several versions of the Preface. This absence, even after what Constant

---

[1] Professor Rigolot's edition, reprinted with corrections in this volume, has provided the basis for our text and most of our annotations. The multiply modified 1635 version had been edited in 1962 by Anne Uildriks, *Les idées littéraires de Mlle de Gournay* (Groningen: Kleine, [1962]), who also printed the 1595 variants, although this volume had a very limited circulation; Olivier Millet's recent collection of texts, *La première réception des Essais de Montaigne (1580-1640)* (Paris: Champion, 1995), includes the 1595 Preface in an edition based on Rigolot's and adds substantial variants from the later versions. Editions, with informative introductions, of the 1599 version (as it was appended to *Le Proumenoir de Monsieur de Montaigne*, 3rd ed.) and of that of 1617 have been produced, respectively, by Anna Lia Franchetti (*Montaigne Studies* 8.1-2 [1996]: 173-192) and Mary McKinley (*Montaigne Studies* 8.1-2 [1996]: 193-219). As Franchetti remarks of the Preface, "Aucun autre texte de Marie de Gournay ne sera repris et remanié autant de fois" [No other text of Marie de Gournay would be taken up again and reworked so many times] ("Marie de Gournay apologiste," 174).

The current revival of interest in all aspects of Marie de Gournay's life and work has led to a 1995 colloquium focusing on her connection with the 1595 edition of the *Essais* (see Jean-Claude Arnould, ed., *Marie de Gournay et l'édition de 1595 des Essais de Montaigne* [Paris: Champion, 1996]), as well as to at least one other conference whose proceedings are now available (Marcel Tetel, ed., *Montaigne and Marie de Gournay, Journal of Medieval and Renaissance Studies* 25 [1995]). Her final (1641) collection of her works, *Les Advis, ou, les Presens de la Demoiselle de Gournay*, is currently being issued in three volumes under the general editorship of Jean-Philippe Beaulieu and Hannah Fournier (Amsterdam and Atlanta, GA: Rodopi, 1997-).

Venesoen terms Marie de Gournay's "exhumation"[2] in the nineteenth century, when her importance for roughly fifty years on the French literary scene became widely recognized, suggests that the modern scholarly concern with textual integrity, as well as with Montaigne's genius, is here at least passively complicit with masculine exclusivity.[3]

When nineteenth-century commentators "exhumed" Marie de Gournay, they imposed on her literary career a configuration into which the Preface does not comfortably fit, and twentieth-century critics—including some with a feminist perspective—have tended to follow suit. The Preface has generally been regarded as an inchoate, indeed incoherent, product of literary "apprenticeship"—a view that, even when coupled with defenses in terms of *écriture féminine*, carries a stigma. To a certain extent, that stigma is shared with the short novel, *Le Proumenoir de Monsieur de Montaigne*, Marie de Gournay's earliest published literary composition (1594) and her only fictional narrative. Although a romantic *histoire tragique* (tragic story) adapted from the second part of the *Discours des Champs faëz* by Claude de Taillemont (1553), *Le Proumenoir* is daringly "realistic" in its treatment of female psychology and sexuality, and is interspersed with digressive reflections, chiefly on the nature of love and relations between the sexes. Stylistically, then, it too is vulnerable to the charge of incoherence. Yet as an avowedly imaginative expression of female experience and perspective, produced in response to a masculinist model, *Le Proumenoir* has proved relatively susceptible to recuperation—to the point of earning consideration as the "'embryon' of the modern novel" (Stanton, "Woman as Object and Subject," 13).[4]

---

[2] See Constant Venesoen, Introd., *Égalité des hommes et des femmes, Grief des dames, Le Proumenoir de Monsieur de Montaigne*, by Marie de Gournay, ed. Constant Venesoen (Geneva: Droz, 1993), 10–11, and Marjorie Henry Ilsley, *A Daughter of the Renaissance: Marie le Jars de Gournay: Her Life and Works* (The Hague: Mouton, 1963), 271ff.; both these authors furnish thorough bibliographies, as does Élyan Dezon-Jones in her anthology of works by Marie de Gournay, *Fragments d'un discours féminin* ([Paris]: Corti, 1988).

[3] There is some reason to suspect that the Preface was dropped—contrary to the tendency of Renaissance translators to include preliminary matter—even by John Florio, when, in 1603, he published the first English translation of the *Essais*. See our translation, n. 3, for a possible indication that Florio knew the Preface of 1595 and hence worked from that edition, rather than from that of 1598, which lacked the Preface. It is demonstrable (see translation, nn. 21 and 101) that he used one of Marie de Gournay's editions, and he is widely presumed to have been at work on the project some years before 1603; Francis A. Yates, e.g., proposes that "he had already started it in 1598, when his [Italian-English] dictionary was published" (*John Florio: The Life of an Italian in Shakespeare's England* [1934; repr. New York: Octagon, 1968], 213).

[4] Domna C. Stanton, "Woman as Object and Subject of Exchange: Marie de Gournay's *Le Proumenoir* (1594)," *L'Esprit créateur* 23.2 (1983): 13. This is to give a feminist twist to the similar claim made by Paul Bonnefon in 1898 but on the patriarchal grounds that the

By contrast, the Preface, in which digressiveness and emotionalism rub shoulders with self-conscious intellectualism and scholarly pretensions, has continued widely to embarrass—a response at least partially anticipated by Marie de Gournay herself. Arguably, however, precisely what the Preface most basically shares with *Le Proumenoir*—a vexed, sometimes vexatious, multivocal comprehensiveness—accords this pair of works, taken together, the status of a watershed in an immensely productive life of writing and feminist commitment.

No doubt, the Marie de Gournay who emerged in later years as a Parisian woman of letters had matters much more under control than previously, both in her life and in her work. A commensurate admiration is evoked from such diverse biographers as Marjorie Henry Ilsley and Élyane Dezon-Jones. Her determination not to marry became increasingly a "given." Despite chronic financial pressures, she progressively achieved a degree of social independence and intellectual respectability, even prominence. She was involved in the founding of the French Academy, the ultimate (though never uncontroversial) intellectual establishment. Her writing, while still pursuing familiar subjects—women's equality, language, morality, religion, education, the life of the mind—and disputatiously engaging in such contemporary questions as the Malherbe-inspired reaction against the Pléiade (a classic case of the new poetics versus the old), became better proportioned, more sharply focused, more easily digestible. She prolifically produced work across a broad range of genres: autobiography, patronage-seeking poetry, translations of the classics, and, of course, essays. Most important, perhaps, her editing and re-editing of Montaigne, while not without its continuing vulnerabilities, now occupied a well-defined niche in her literary life; her position as "fille d'alliance" seems to have become less of a burden.

Such developments lend themselves, perhaps rather too readily, to teleological narratives of maturity and accomplishment. Tilde A. Sankovitch, pursuing the thesis that Marie de Gournay mythologizes herself

---

novel was in fact the child of *Montaigne*'s modernism, "composé sous les yeux du philosophe, sinon avec son assentiment" [composed under the eyes of the philosopher, if not with his approval] (*Montaigne et ses amis: La Boétie, Charron, Mlle de Gournay* [1898; repr. Geneva: Slatkine, 1969], 2: 325). The metaphor used by Stanton and Bonnefon plays on the fact that the novel's heroine brings about the death of herself and her unborn child; cf. Constant Venesoen, *Études sur la littérature féminine au XVIIe siècle* (Birmingham, AL: Summa, 1990): "... c'est aussi, symboliquement, l'immolation d'un fantasme créateur qui, contre le père adoptif, s'est complu dans l'éros séducteur" [... it is also, symbolically, the immolation of a fantasy of creation that, going against the adoptive father, has satisfied itself in seductive *eros*] (23).

as an androgynous epic hero, considers that the filial ambivalence evident in *Le Proumenoir* (she does not mention the Preface) is "fully resolved":

> After Montaigne's death, Marie de Gournay finds it possible to become her own champion, and to complete, once and for all, her journey toward her constantly pursued and constant self.[5]

By a more strictly literary route, Ilsley arrives in due course at a similar destination—"The Golden Years" (*Daughter of the Renaissance*, 242-265), which she figures metonymically in terms of stylistic fulfilment: Marie de Gournay "gained perspective on the past without abandoning its riches and beauty and without ever attaining a classical clarity" (244). This phase is marked, in Ilsley's view, by a mellow "mingling of modern tendencies, where her prose has gained in clarity, with passages in which she retained her earlier style and favorite archaisms" (244). A superficial contrast exists between such a perspective and that of Dezon-Jones, who, anthologizing (mainly) the later feminist and autobiographical works under the rubric of *Fragments d'un discours féminin*, insists on discursive fragmentation as the basic character of Marie de Gournay's writing throughout her life. Even Dezon-Jones, however, is led to speak of the "unité secrète" [secret unity] of *L'Ombre de la damoiselle de Gournay*—the intriguingly entitled ("ombre" = "shadow") penultimate collection of her works (1626)[6]—albeit that unity consists of a "mise en accusation kaléidoscopique du langage en tant que moyen de communication, alors que les hommes s'en servent comme instrument d'oppression" [a kaleidoscopic arraignment of language as a means of communication, while men use it as an instrument of oppression] (Introd., *Discours féminin*, 80). Elsewhere, the same commentator chronicles "le glissement progressif des techniques autobiographiques vers une méthode de l'autoportrait" [the progressive sliding of autobiographical techniques towards a method of self-portraiture][7]—a point of convergence, in a surprising way, with Sankovitch, who devotes much

---

[5] Tilde A. Sankovitch, *French Women Writers and the Book: Myths of Access and Desire* (Syracuse, NY: Syracuse University Press, 1988), 82-83.

[6] With Dezon-Jones' approach to the "shadow," cf. the remark of Pierre Villey (echoing Mario Schiff): "Par la grande Préface de 1595, Marie de Gournay s'installe pour la vie à l'ombre du grand Montaigne" [With the long Preface of 1595, Marie de Gournay situates herself for the term of her life in the shadow of the great Montaigne] (*Montaigne devant la postérité* [Paris: Ancienne Librairie Furne, Boivin, (1935)], 46).

[7] Élyane Dezon-Jones, "Marie de Gournay: le je/u/ palimpseste," *L'Esprit créateur* 23.2 (1983), 36.

attention to the writer's self-representations (focusing especially on the poetic character-portrait entitled "Peincture de moeurs").[8]

To recover the significance of the Preface requires resisting teleology, whether "conservative" or "radical." Nevertheless, we must reckon with the fact that Marie de Gournay herself was the one who, in response to hostile reaction, initially severed the connection between her text and that of Montaigne. The connection was to be renewed in the editions of 1617, 1625, and 1635, for which (on the model of Montaigne's own practice) Marie de Gournay provided successively revised versions—truncated in some respects, elongated in others—of the original Preface.[9] Her second edition of 1598, however, set the stage for the perfunctory Prefaces to intervening editions by radically substituting a brief retraction, in which she disclaimed her capacity to write about the *Essais* and meekly deferred to her readers' opinions. Such an abrupt reversal of her original attitude—for in 1595 she hardly backed off from telling the public what to think—may be taken to mark increased professionalism and maturity. But it also smacks of inner conflict, especially given her explicit avowal of "faiblesse" [weakness].

That term and concept are clearly gendered, and they recur throughout Marie de Gournay's *oeuvre*, beginning with the 1595 Preface itself. There they figure in a strong feminist refutation of male claims to rational superiority: even a man who fails to pursue an argument with a woman because he is "stymied half-way by his own feebleness [*foiblesse*] ... will be termed at once victorious and courteous" (see translation, 37). The attack on the common presumption of female weakness is carried over into those considerably later treatises on feminist themes for which Marie de Gournay is chiefly known today: *Égalité des hommes et des femmes* (1622) and *Grief des dames* (1626).[10] In this light, for her

---

[8] The surprise stems from the fundamental opposition between the fragmentational approach of Dezon-Jones and the unitary one of Sankovitch; the latter goes so far as to assert that "there is no sense of interior combat, no *déchirement* [anguish] in Marie de Gournay" (*French Women Writers*, 89).

[9] For accounts of the Prefaces to successive editions of the *Essais*, see Villey, *Montaigne devant la postérité*, 50–51; Ilsley, *Daughter of the Renaissance*, 61 n. 2; Rigolot, Introd., "Préface à l'édition des *Essais* de Montaigne," by Marie le Jars de Gournay, *Montaigne Studies* 1 (1989): 11–13; Franchetti, "Marie de Gournay apologiste," 172–177; and McKinley, "Revival," 193–201, in addition to Millet's variorum edition of the Preface. For precise bibliographical descriptions of the editions themselves, see Richard A. Sayce and David Maskell, *A Descriptive Bibliography of Montaigne's* Essais, *1580–1700* (London: The Bibliographical Society and The Modern Humanities Research Association, 1983).

[10] It is important to judge Marie de Gournay's feminist writings, whose importance and originality have been much debated, against the background of the long-standing "Querelle des Femmes" [Woman Controversy]—see Ilsley, *Daughter of the Renaissance*, 200–216; Ian

to cite her "faiblesse" as an impediment to commenting on Montaigne suggests that the point of real sensitivity for Marie de Gournay was less her feminist convictions in themselves than their—and her own—association with her "father."

At virtually the same time that the 1595 Preface was being suppressed in one place, an abridged version of it re-surfaced in another—as an adjunct to the third edition (1599) of *Le Proumenoir*.[11] This was at once to distance it from Montaigne and to renew the connection with him. The full title of Marie de Gournay's novel memorializes its origin in conversation between the "father" and "daughter" during his lengthy visit to her family home at Gournay-sur-Aronde (in Picardy) during the autumn of 1588. She wrote the novel and sent him the manuscript shortly after his departure, but there is no record of any response on his part, and she recovered it only in early 1594, when Montaigne's widow and the poet Pierre de Brach forwarded it to her in Paris, together with the corrected copy of the *Essais* on which she would base her edition. Montaigne is present, not only in the title and the dedicatory epistle, but in the text itself, addressed by the narrator at highly charged moments, such as when the heroine's illicit love-longings are vividly evoked: "Toutefois, ce n'est pas mon gibier d'escrire le progrez de son amour, mon pere, il me suffit de le plaindre" [However, it is not my object to write about the progress of her love, father; it is enough for me to pity it] (Venesoen, ed., 116). All in all, there is good reason to accept Venesoen's judgment about the bearing of Marie de Gournay's youthful fiction on the same psychological issue that pervasively informs the Preface:[12]

> Il lève un voile sur la sensibilité de Marie de Gournay, sur sa perception même de cette relation de "fille" à "père" qu'elle

---

Maclean, *Woman Triumphant: Feminism in French Literature 1610–1652* (Oxford: Clarendon Press, 1977), 25–63; and Maïté Albistur and Daniel Armogathe, *Histoire du féminisme français du moyen âge à nos jours* ([Paris]: Éditions Des Femmes, 1977), 1: 174–188; cf. also Venesoen, *Études*.

[11] On the 1599 version of the Preface and its "prehistory," see Franchetti, "Marie de Gournay apologiste." Cf. Villey's speculation about Marie de Gournay's inability to sacrifice "un morceau d'éloquence qui a coûté tant de peines: auquel on a confié tant de ses ambitions" [a piece of eloquence which cost such efforts, to which were entrusted so many of her ambitions] (*Montaigne devant la postérité*, 48).

[12] Such acceptance does not require endorsing Venesoen's skepticism about Marie de Gournay's credentials as a significant feminist intellectual. Apart from the Introduction to his edition, see also his *Études*, esp. 17–42, where a psychoanalytic reading of *Le Proumenoir* and the possibility of granting such credentials—as most contemporary critics would readily do—again seem unnecessarily opposed.

avait entretenue avec l'auteur des *Essais*, sur le degré de dépendance vis-à-vis de Montaigne, qu'elle était prête à concéder; enfin, sur sa propre destinée de femme, peu encline à partager la vision virile, voire misogyne,—malgré Montaigne!—du monde qui l'entourait.

[It sheds light on the sensitivity of Marie de Gournay, even on her perception of that relation of "daughter" to "father" which she had maintained with the author of the *Essais*; on the degree of dependence with regard to Montaigne that she was prepared to concede; finally, on her own destiny as a woman, little inclined to share the masculine, indeed misogynist vision—despite Montaigne!—of the world that surrounded her.] (Introd., 73)

It is by way of the issues of identity and voice that such a personal reading of Marie de Gournay's literary production in these early years of her extensive career may most readily be squared with the predominantly social and political perspective of such commentators as Cathleen M. Bauschatz and Dezon-Jones. The former has focused on the Preface as a site of "struggle for self-definition in relation to the father, who is revered and yet who causes anxiety."[13] The latter, speaking of *Le Proumenoir*, considers that "[d]ans l'écriture, le rapport de Marie de Gournay à Montaigne demeure particulièrement ambigu" [(i)n the process of writing, the relation of Marie de Gournay to Montaigne remains especially ambiguous] (Introd., *Discours féminin*, 22);[14] indeed, Dezon-Jones discerns—and it is difficult to miss—a strong tinge of masochism in the dedicatory epistle:

encore ne sais–je si je ne prends pas volontiers plaisir à faire quelque niaiserie exprès pour vous mettre, en me châtiant, mon

---

[13] Cathleen M. Bauschatz, "Imitation, Writing, and Self-Study in Marie de Gournay's 1595 'Préface' to Montaigne's *Essais*," in *Contending Kingdoms: Historical, Psychological, and Feminist Approaches to the Literature of Sixteenth-Century England and France*, ed. Marie-Rose Logan and Peter L. Rudnytsky, 346–364 (Detroit, MI: Wayne State University Press, 1991), 349. Bauschatz has also written about the Preface as "the first literary critical reading of the *Essais*" ("Marie de Gournay's 'Préface de 1595': A Critical Evaluation," *Bulletin de la Société des Amis de Montaigne* 3-4 [1986]: 82).

[14] Cf. Stanton, who documents the ambiguity that can occur when the novel's heroine is addressing *her* "père" ("Woman as Object and Subject," 21), and Patricia Francis Cholakian, Introd., *Le Proumenoir de Monsieur de Montaigne (1594): A Facsimile Reproduction* (Delmar, NY: Scholars' Facsimiles and Reprints, 1985), esp. 19–20. On the dedicatory epistle's evident "ambiguity," see also Maryanne Cline Horowitz, "Marie de Gournay, Editor of the *Essais* of Michel de Montaigne: A Case-Study in Mentor-Protégée Friendship," *Sixteenth Century Journal* 17 (1986): 280.

père, à l'exercice de l'empire que vous avez en moi.

[I still do not know whether I am not willingly taking pleasure in deliberately producing a certain silliness in order to induce you, father, to exercise, in correcting/punishing me, the dominion that you possess over me.]
            (cited Dezon-Jones, Introd., *Discours féminin*, 22)[15]

Inevitably, this self-chastising impulse offers to help explain the fact that, even though *Le Proumenoir* achieved considerable popularity, it, too, underwent successive "softening"[16] excisions, modifications, and supplementations in the five editions that followed its first appearance. The 1599 version, for example, while appending the abridged 1595 Preface, dropped a thirty-four-page digression in which Marie de Gournay had vigorously pursued her preoccupations with women's lack of education and male inconstancy. Montaigne's posthumous influence may well have been at work: much as the "daughter" liked to believe that her feminist themes were in sympathy with the views of her "father," the evidence of the *Essays*, as scholars generally agree, was against her.

The idea of "adoption" between intellectuals, not uncommon in sixteenth-century Europe, had more of "literary partnership" (Ilsley, *Daughter of the Renaissance*, 31) about it than we might assume today. By the same token, literary partnership tended to be more personally charged, thanks largely to the pervasive Neoplatonism that idealized friendship as spiritual union—a preoccupation of Marie de Gournay in both *Le Proumenoir* and the Preface. Given Marie de Gournay's imaginative intensity, as well as the boundaries of age, gender, and status involved, her "adoptive" position *vis-à-vis* Montaigne could hardly fail

---

[15] Cf. John Donne's "Holy Sonnet 14," lines 7–14, in which the speaker implores God's love in the form of punishment for his reason's sinful lapses:

> Reason your viceroy in mee, mee should defend,
> But is captiv'd, and proves weake or untrue.
> Yet dearly'I love you, 'and would be loved faine,
> But am betroth'd unto your enemie:
> Divorce mee, 'untie, or breake that knot againe,
> Take mee to you, imprison me, for I
> Except you'enthrall mee, never shal be free,
> Nor ever chast, except you ravish me.
>   (*The Complete Poetry of John Donne*, ed. John T. Shawcross
>   [Garden City, NY: Doubleday Anchor, 1967])

[16] Ilsley's term (*Daughter of the Renaissance*, 59). Cf. Cholakian, Introd., *Le Proumenoir*, 35–40 on the revisions as Montaigne-like yet involving "a never-ending attempt to please her male colleagues and her 'father's' ghost" (35), as well as to establish a place for female desire.

to catalyze tensions affecting not only the matter but the manner of her discourse. Those tensions may themselves be roughly figured within the Renaissance Neoplatonic framework (not to mention the Christian one, since "mon père" is also the form of address for a priest). Yet they also lend themselves fruitfully to psychological treatment, especially feminist psychoanalysis.[17] And from this point of view, it is even less surprising to find the role of "daughter" surcharged with affect after the death of the "father," since mourning typically activates ambivalence and renders a dependent identity precarious.

Obviously, the complex textual web that Marie de Gournay wove, unwove, and rewove round herself and Montaigne with special intensity during the mid and late 1590s originated in an unusual set of personal circumstances (albeit combined with common social conditions). Yet we may also discern a pattern that has since been widely recognized as typical of the Early Modern period—namely, the construction and representation of the self in relation to what psychoanalysis terms the Other. Marie de Gournay was arguably ahead of her time, not only in her social and political opinions, but as a public model of emergent subjectivity. This element appears more strikingly by way of what might appear, at first glance, a far-fetched comparison. There is a remarkable affinity between Marie de Gournay's (inter)textual negotiation of identity, especially in the "mourning period" from which the Preface emerged, and the quintessentially "modern" self-struggle of a near-contemporary (roughly 1600) fictional personage, Shakespeare's Hamlet—a figure regularly cited by historians of subjectivity as marking a shift in the cultural paradigm. The play's "self-unfolding" protagonist begins from a conflicted position analogous to that of the Preface's author and heroine—at once newly bereft of a father and "too much in the sun" (1.2.67).[18] Indeed, allowing for the difference in gender, the famous pun in the latter statement uncannily conveys Marie de Gournay's sense of herself as both uncomfortably exposed and sheltered (or trapped) within her father's shadow.

Such comparison with Shakespeare's play tends to confirm that the

---

[17] See, notably, Stanton on "the problematics of the female subject" ("Woman as Object and Subject," 23) in *Le Proumenoir*.
[18] *The Riverside Shakespeare*, gen eds. G. Blakemore Evans and J.J.M. Tobin, 2nd ed. (Boston: Houghton Mifflin, 1997). I have more fully explored this affinity in an article ("*Hamlet* et la Préface de Marie de Gournay," *Renaissance and Reformation/Renaissance et Réforme* n.s. 18 [1994]: 29–42) and in my book, *Self-Speaking in Medieval and Early Modern English Drama: Subjectivity, Discourse and the Stage* (Basingstoke, Hampshire: Macmillan; New York: St. Martin's, 1997), 270–279.

Preface is significant as a cultural, not merely a personal, document. That argument has hitherto been made only in terms of gender—in particular, the challenge faced by "une femme qui parle" [a woman speaking] (see translation, 35) in a largely hostile masculine milieu. The question of female speech may be broadened, however, by reading gender as, at least in part, a property of the "self" as discursively formulated, hence an aspect of the larger problematic of the speaking subject. In fact, justification for this move may be found in Hamlet's own practice of defining himself in relation to the feminine—a practice that begins with aggressive contempt for the "[f]railty"—that is, *faiblesse*—whose "name is woman" (1.2.146) and ends with a guarded acknowledgment of "such a kind of gain-giving, as would perhaps trouble a woman" (5.2.214-215).[19] With regard to Marie de Gournay's career, such a perspective might effect a *rapprochement* between the divergent perspectives of Dezon-Jones and Venesoen—that is, between, respectively, foregrounding gender issues and assimilating them to the human condition at large.

In turn, invoking the model of Hamlet may illuminate the contradictory and ambivalent attitudes typified by such earlier commentators as Mario Schiff and Alan M. Boase, who sometimes seem to combine in their portrayals of Marie de Gournay the traditional positive and negative "takes" on Shakespeare's character—that is, as either thwarted hero or ineffectual neurotic.[20] For Schiff, Marie de Gournay "se jeta courageusement dans la mêlée littéraire et s'égara même par instants dans la politique" [threw herself courageously into the literary fray and even strayed from time to time into the political arena] (*Marie de Gournay*, 24); yet, given her modest and uneven talents, her emotional excess and eccentricities rendered her liable to mockery, against which she lacked even the defense of beauty (37)—"même cette beauté fugitive et légère dont le diable s'est fait le parrain" [even that fugitive and delicate beauty of which the devil has made himself the godfather] (1). Venesoen is putting it mildly when he observes that Schiff "ne semble pas avoir eu beaucoup de sympathie pour le sujet de son livre" [does not seem to have had much sympathy for the subject of his book] (*Études*, 20). The same might finally be said of Boase, who applies the reason-passion dichotomy rather more subtly (since he wants Marie de Gournay to repre-

---

[19] The self-feminization associated with inward conflict in the sonnet of Donne cited above (n. 15) may be read similarly.

[20] Mario Schiff, *La fille d'alliance de Montaigne, Marie de Gournay* (1910; repr. Geneva: Slatkine, 1978); Alan M. Boase, *The Fortunes of Montaigne: A History of the* Essais *in France, 1580–1669* (1935; repr. New York: Octagon, 1970).

sent a "purely rationalistic humanism" [*Fortunes of Montaigne*, 72]), but with more active condescension: she had, it seems, only "a small stock of reasoned ideas which she set forth with considerable force and acumen, if, alas! with little literary skill" (48). The question of literary skill lets the stereotypical emotional female in by the back door: "It is only, however, when Marie loses her temper that she is readable" (57). Boase's patronizing recourse to the first name here confirms his statement's affinity with that traditional masculine deflective maneuver, "You're so pretty when you're angry!"

To refigure the essential issue as subjectivity itself is further to resist a teleological reading of Marie de Gournay's career. For in this light the stubbornly discontinuous and stylistically phantasmagoric writings of Marie de Gournay's formative years—notably, *Le Proumenoir* and the Preface—effectively recuperate the chaotic and subversive dimension that remained attached to her "mature" identity as a woman of letters. The scorn and ridicule that she continually attracted from much of the male literary establishment—Philippe Desan reports that "no one was the subject of more mockery than she was during the seventeenth century"[21] —extended to bizarre practical jokes, her stigmatization as nostalgically resisting the evolution of the French language, and even her appearance as a character in a satirical comedy. Certainly, these elements need no longer condition her biography, as they seem to have done for Bonnefon ("l'âge augmentait son obstination et ses ridicules" [age increased her obstinacy and her absurdities] [*Montaigne et ses amis*, 365]). But they need to be recognized as continuing in her public image just what Rigolot finds most striking about the Preface as a literary project— namely, "un double discours: celui de la défense de Montaigne et celui de sa propre légitimation" [a double discourse: that of the defense of Montaigne and that of her own legitimation] (Introd., 17). Such a reading makes for a direct connection between the early work and the later life, notably as characterized by Boase:

> Till the end of her life we find a double chorus of fantastic stories about the tricks played on her, and her eccentricities, and, on the other hand, the most hyperbolical praises of her learning.
> (*Fortunes of Montaigne*, 53)[22]

---

[21] Philippe Desan, "The Book, the Friend, the Woman: Montaigne's Circular Exchanges," trans. Brad Bassler, in *Contending Kingdoms: Historical, Psychological, and Feminist Approaches to the Literature of Sixteenth-Century England and France*, ed. Marie-Rose Logan and Peter L. Rudnytsky, 225–262 (Detroit, MI: Wayne State University Press, 1991), 257.

[22] One of the most intriguing non-literary features of Marie de Gournay's life—her

Rigolot's notion of "un double discours" is refreshingly legitimizing. Pierre Villey, the eminent pioneer of modern Montaigne scholarship, memorably registered the same perception some time ago in terms of the encroachment upon Marie de Gournay's homage to Montaigne of an out-of-control justification of herself "[d]ans l'ivresse du triomphe, et sous le fouet des sarcasmes" [(i)n the drunkenness of her triumph and under the lash of sarcastic attacks] (*Montaigne devant la postérité*, 42). The Preface, in his view, is finally a "pauvre chose" [wretched thing] (42) because "[à] chaque instant elle s'évade, en longues digressions, du premier sujet dans le second" [(a)t every moment she takes flight, in long digressions, from the first subject into the second] (43).[23] Her subsequent subordination of herself to Montaigne is key to the esteem that Villey finally accords her: she earned the right to restore her Preface to the 1617 edition of the *Essais* (albeit in a version thoroughly purged of excess and excrescence) because "[e]lle s'était remise à sa tâche d'éditeur" [(s)he had reapplied herself to her job as editor] (50). Yet the "deux mérites" [two merits] that Villey allows her—zealous service to Montaigne's memory and understanding of his originality—must still, for him, be disengaged from the heap of mockeries "qu'elle accumulait sur sa tête" [that she accumulated upon her head] (51), to which Marie de Gournay was doomed by the same innate defect that vitiated the first Preface: "son superbe manque de mesure et de goût" [her superb lack of moderation and taste] (53).

At the least, the dimension of ridicule, which can hardly be excluded from the picture of Marie de Gournay's career, may be productively accommodated insofar as it remains inscribed in her work. Such is perhaps most dramatically (if not necessarily most directly) the case with the 1616 autobiography that she was duped into writing on the pretext that King James I of England wished her do to so.[24] It seems impor-

---

enthusiasm for alchemy, which she pursued to the detriment of her finances, as well as her reputation—lent itself at the time, and still does, to precisely this double perspective: it was associated, on the one hand, with charlatanism and gullibility (as in Ben Jonson's *The Alchemist*), on the other, thanks to Neoplatonism, with arcane knowledge of the secret powers of nature. This latter point is pushed especially hard by Sankovitch, who celebrates Marie de Gournay as, in her experiments, "enacting or reenacting the process of her own becoming as . . . she achieves the transmutation into the self whose promise, like that of the philosopher's stone, the *Essays* had held out to her" (*French Women Writers*, 83). One feels that a touch of Jonsonian scepticism might be in order here.

[23] Despite his narrow perspective, Villey's brief summary of the Preface (*Montaigne devant la postérité*, 42–46) displays a characteristic incisiveness.

[24] She eventually chose to publish this work in *Les Advis, ou, les Presens de la Demoiselle de Gournay* (1641).

tant, moreover, to attach that dimension to such undoubtedly rebarbative and provocative elements as her avowed thirst for fame, her penchant for pointed attacks, her fragile sense of proportion, and her plain lapses of judgment (the very faculty most exalted in the Preface—in the name, needless to say, of Montaigne). These qualities point backwards, towards the early writings, by way of their self-subverting tendency, as when she coupled her published laments for the 1610 assassination of Henri IV—clearly a patronage-driven appeal for favor—with an incredibly impolitic justification of the Jesuits, who were widely held responsible for the deed.[25] (*Défense des pères Jésuites* is one work she never republished.) Even the questions, so urgent in the Preface and *Le Proumenoir*, of voice and identity *vis-à-vis* an intellectual "father" are renewed *sotto voce*, as it were, by way of her partial rewriting in 1624 of Ronsard's poem, "La Harangue du Duc de Guise aux soldats de Metz"—an intervention rendered more problematic (and inviting hostility) by her fraudulent gift of the piece to the king as representing the poet's own latest revisions.[26] In sum, a case can be made that the conspicuous contradictions and excesses of the youthful Marie de Gournay by no means evaporate but rather diffuse their energy by flowing into a variety of (mostly) quieter channels.

An important consideration for a reader of these early works (and certainly an inescapable one for translators of the Preface) is that the qualities in question are discursive ones—"[d]ans l'écriture," to return to the formulation of Dezon-Jones. From this angle, the remarks made by Rigolot in the Introduction originally provided for his edition are especially pertinent and worth citing at some length. From the basic notion of the "double discours," Rigolot derives a psychoanalytic reading, along the lines we have already explored, of the conflicted relation between the "adoptive daughter" and her "father":

Dans la mesure où il autorise sa "fille" à mettre en lumière les

---

[25] In fact, Marie de Gournay may have had prior information about the assassination, including the involvement of persons in high places (Ilsley, *Daughter of the Renaissance*, 116-118; Dezon-Jones, Introd., *Discours féminin*, 40-41).

[26] Whereas Bonnefon wrote an account of this incident as simply a "supercherie" [fraud] ("Une supercherie de Mlle de Gournay," *Revue d'histoire littéraire de la France* 3 [1896]: 71-89), both Ilsley, *Daughter of the Renaissance*, 137, and Dezon-Jones, Introd., *Discours féminin*, 77-78, explain it, in part, by invoking Marie de Gournay's devotion to modernizing the French language. Even Montaigne's own language, so vigorously defended in the Preface, eventually came in for some updating at her hands (Boase, *Fortunes of Montaigne*, 63), although Villey (*Montaigne devant la postérité*, 52) usefully places this fact in the context of contemporary editorial practices.

> derniers avatars de son écriture, le "père" confère en principe toutes les garanties de sérieux à la nouvelle édition. Mais, en même temps, parce que le "père" demande à sa "fille" de parler pour *lui* et non pour *elle*, c'est seulement à travers les intérêts du surmoi paternel que peut se faire reconnaître l'identité de la "fille d'alliance." Cette "liaison," qui se poursuit au delà de la mort du père pour déterminer l'identité de la fille, constitue ainsi à la fois une promesse de plénitude et un danger d'aliénation.

[Insofar as he authorizes his "daughter" to make public the most recent incarnations of his writing, the "father" fully guarantees in principle the weight carried by the new edition. But, at the same time, because the "father" asks his "daughter" to speak for *him*, and not for *her*, the identity of the "adoptive daughter" can gain recognition only by cutting across the interests of the paternal superego. This "relationship," which perpetuates itself beyond the father's death to determine the identity of the daughter, thus constitutes at once a promise of plenitude and a danger of alienation.] (17)

Even more to the point, Rigolot goes on to trace some of the stylistic ramifications of this discursive "doublure" [doubling/lining]. Most basically, this "long texte complexe et touffu" [long, complex, and dense text] (14) is distinguished by its elaborate, often convoluted, language, which, however, is not "gratuite" [gratuitous] but rather

> découle, en fait, des contraintes qu'impose cette ambiguïté rhétorique et qui motivent le recours a l'hypotactisme, à l'amplification et aux ruptures de construction. Les longues phrases, à subordonnées multiples ou coupées de parenthèses et d'incisives, servent à véhiculer la duplicité d'une pensée écartelée entre des sollicitations divergentes. L'abondance des tours elliptiques, les changements brusques de construction (anacoluthes) et la suppression des liaisons phrastiques (asyndètes) obligent le lecteur à entrer dans le labyrinthe d'une écriture traversée par les reprises et les repentirs, et qui n'est pas sans rappeler celle de Montaigne.

[flows, in fact, from the constraints imposed by this rhetorical ambiguity and which account for the recourse to hypotaxis, to amplification, and to ruptures of construction. The long sentences, made up of multiple subordinations or cut by parentheses

and insertions, serve to convey the duplicity of a thought-process torn by divergent demands. The abundance of elliptical phrasings, the abrupt changes of construction (anacoluthon), and the suppression of conjunctions (asyndeton) force the reader into the labyrinth of a mode of writing shot through with fresh starts and second thoughts, and which is not without resemblance to that of Montaigne.] (18)

It would be difficult to produce a more precise summary of the general stylistic character of the Preface, or to indicate more clearly the formidable technical problems that it poses for translators. As for the reminiscences of Montaigne, they are naturally pervasive, not only in the mode of composition but in phraseology and ideas, and the combined annotations of the editor and the translators can hardly pretend to have documented all of them. Fortunately, many of the other points singled out by Rigolot—the plethora of paradox, the vivid imagery (by which all of Marie de Gournay's writing is characterized),[27] the qualities of *varietas* and *festivitas* (19), "la finesse et la vigueur" [the subtlety and force] (16) of the arguments advanced on behalf of Montaigne—point to ways in which her prose sometimes, on the contrary, virtually translates itself, and gives pleasure in the process.

A particular challenge involving tone and vocabulary relates to two categories of tendentious usage whose very coexistence sustains the "*dédoublement intentionnel*" [split orientation] (Rigolot, Introd., 17) of Marie de Gournay. First, there are the socially fraught terms of approval and abuse that she uses so liberally in criticizing contemporary manners and morals, especially with regard to literary judgment and the attitudes of men to women. These include (on the positive side) "galland homme" and "suffisance"/"suffisant," to which we draw attention in the notes; on the negative side, "fat," for which we have preferred "poseur" to the dictionary's usual "fop"—a term current in Elizabethan English in a cognate sense but whose associations for modern English speakers have been skewed by later usage (and attitudes towards "effeminacy"). "Poseur," for English speakers today, comes closer to conveying the kind of social and intellectual pretentiousness that Marie de Gournay was targeting. The other problematic category of terms involves those whose Neoplatonic resonances resist the literal, the concrete, and the

---

[27] For stimulating insight into her critical views on this subject, see Peggy P. Holmes, "Mlle de Gournay's Defence of Baroque Imagery," *French Studies* 8 (1954): 122–131.

present: "belle ame" (we have settled on—or for—"rare spirit"); "grand esprit" ("great mind"). Nowhere is the "doublure" of Marie de Gournay's discourse more evident than in her deployment of these two linguistic registers—often in the same (usually long) breath—to distinguish, broadly speaking, the way things are from the way they should be.

At the two extremities of style associated with this dualism—extremities which, moreover, are often juxtaposed or intermixed, and which typically draw heavily on the most elusive sectors of her vocabulary—translation faces its greatest challenges. Colette Quesnel and I would not claim to have met all the challenges successfully, but neither have we wished to efface them, since they stem in large measure from conflicts that profoundly inform the original. For this reason, we would like our readers to take our text less as a clear window on Marie de Gournay's ideas and arguments than as a record of our sometimes frustrating—but often exhilarating—engagement with the turbulence, both stylistic and intellectual, that is generated by those conflicts.

We feel, moreover, that by giving full tonal weight to Marie de Gournay's positive and negative "excesses," translation may, paradoxically, highlight the fact that neither Marie de Gournay's critique of reality nor her idealism is a simple matter. This point has sometimes been obscured in biographical commentaries. Naturally, Marie de Gournay's feminism, maintained throughout her life, is usually taken as the central pillar of her political thought. The questions of statecraft and class-relations, however, on which she soon became notably more moderate (insofar as may be judged from her writing),[28] may provide more immediate access to the complicating effect that her "*dédoublement intentionnel*" has even on her attitude to male-female relations. On the one hand, her satirical assault on the snobbish and fat-headed nobleman, anxious to collect a sight of a great man for fashion's sake but normally not deigning to notice his inferiors ("When someone consorts only with the nobly born, it is a sign that noble birth is all he has" [translation, 87]), accords with the quasi-radicalism of the social and political attitudes originally incorporated in *Le Proumenoir*. On the other hand, the Preface is full of contemptuous references to the vulgar "foulle d'aveugles" [crowd of the blind], and on at least one occasion, she allusively skews Montaigne in a distinctly less egalitarian direction (see translation, nn. 89 and 92). Arguably, the key to this apparent conflict is furnished by her

---

[28] See Ilsley's account (*Daughter of the Renaissance*, 91) of the changes to *Le Proumenoir* in this regard, beginning in 1599.

assertion that "the common people and the vulgar extend so far that in any state there are fewer who are not vulgar than there are princes" (translation, 23). The concept of vulgarity is thereby shifted in register from concrete to abstract.

Early Modern moral satire, when it is not "purely" anti-feminist, frequently uses the figure of Woman to exemplify in extreme form the weaknesses and corrupt tendencies of human beings generally: their passions, their vanity, their hypocrisy. As a basic strategy, Marie de Gournay inverts this procedure, using her position as a privileged intellectual woman—privileged not necessarily by her education (which she had to gain on her own with great exertion) but by her "alliance" with Montaigne—in order to expose the follies of the "vulgar," in whatever social station the latter are to be found. She can do this not only because she excites the dismissive contempt of innumerable "fats"—men obviously inferior both to herself and to Montaigne—but also because she can thus better perceive the true weaknesses of most women, which she has no difficulty in acknowledging, since these are to be blamed on ignorance. It follows that the standard satirical perspective, according to which glorious antiquity is praised by contrast with the degenerate present, is transformed into an ideal of equality amongst "grands esprits," masculine as well as feminine.

It is, perhaps, as a necessary pivotal move in this process that the "androgyny" perceived by Sankovitch and others comes most convincingly into play. Marie de Gournay and Montaigne, as "semblables" ("like spirits"), are assimilated in quasi-mythic form to the ancient model. In this process—and in the linguistic exaltation that enacts it— there are strong traces of the Neoplatonic ideal of the transcendental union of reason and passion, even as there are inevitable traces of that ideal's unattainability. Marie de Gournay is quite capable of exercising Aristotelian logic in thoroughly reasoned and straightforward language, although at the same time, for tactical reasons, she may ironically represent herself as an *ingénue*. But her prose is also rife with effusions of idealized feeling—often in extended, extravagant, even ambiguous phrases, which effectively celebrate their own impulsiveness. Such phrases are ultimately best understood less as eccentricities than as verbal reflections of the impulse to renew and revalidate the spiritual communion of "daughter" and "father"—an impulse of which Marie de Gournay herself is at once object and subject.

Richard Hillman
The University of Western Ontario

Translators' Explanatory Note

The footnotes in the English translation are based on, and in part translated from, those supplied by François Rigolot for the French edition. The original annotation has been largely adapted and supplemented, however, and the translators accept responsibility for any errors of fact or judgment thereby introduced.

The edition of Montaigne's *Essais* referred to in the notes to the translation is that of Pierre Villey, new ed. with a Preface by V.-L. Saulnier (Paris: Presses Universitaires de France, 1965), which is cited by book, chapter, and page numbers, with the letters A, B, and C designating, respectively, the redaction of 1580, that of 1588, and later manuscript additions. References (by volume and page numbers) are also provided to the corresponding passages in *Montaigne's Essays*, trans. John Florio (1603), with an Introd. by L. C. Harmer, 3 vols., Everyman's Library (London: Dent; New York: Dutton, 1965). More strictly accurate modern translations, based on more reliable editions, are, of course, available, but Florio's, which may actually follow Marie de Gournay's edition of 1595, will be of particular interest to readers of her Preface.

PREFACE SUR LES ESSAIS DE MICHEL SEIGNEUR DE MONTAIGNE,
Par sa Fille d'Alliance.

Si vous demandez à quelque artisan, quel est Cæsar, il vous respondra que c'est un excellent Capitaine. Si vous le luy montrez luy-mesme sans nom avec ces grandes parties par lesquelles il l'estoit, sa suffisance, labeur, vigilance, perseverance, ordre, art de mesnager le temps et de se faire aymer et craindre, sa resolution et ses admirables conseils sur les nouvelles et promtes occurrences; si, dis je, apres luy avoir fait contempler toutes ces choses, vous luy demandez quel homme c'est là, certes il le vous donnera volontiers pour l'un des fuyards de la bataille de Pharsale: parce que, pour juger d'un grand Capitaine, il faut l'estre soy-mesme ou capable de le devenir par instruction[1]. Il ne sert guere à un Athlete de monstrer la force et vigueur de ses membres à quelque cheval, pour luy faire croire qu'il emportera le prix de la lucte, puis qu'il est incapable de sentir si c'est par les cheveux qu'il s'y faut prendre. Enquerez semblablement cet homme, ce qu'il luy semble de Platon, il vous remplira l'oreille des loüanges d'un celeste Philosophe;

---

[1] Sur la page de garde des *Commentarii* de Jules César, qu'il possédait, Montaigne avait noté «la grandeur incomparable de cette âme». Cf. *Essais,* éd. P. Villey, tome I, p. XLV, note 1. (Nos références aux *Essais* de Montaigne se rapportent à l'édition de Pierre Villey en trois volumes [Paris, Presses Universitaires de France, 1988]. Nous donnons désormais le livre en chiffre romain, suivi du chapitre et de la page en chiffres arabes. Les lettres A, B, et C renvoient aux trois principales couches de texte [1580, 1588 et 1595].) La bataille de Pharsale décida de la victoire de César sur Pompée (48 av. J.-C.). Montaigne en fait huit fois mention dans les *Essais*.

PREFACE TO THE *ESSAYS* OF MICHEL DE MONTAIGNE by his Adoptive Daughter.

If you ask any artisan who Caesar was, he will tell you: an excellent commander. If you present him anonymously with the man as he was, with those great qualities that gained him that status—his ability, hard work, vigilance, perseverance, organization, skill in managing time and in making himself loved and feared, his resolution and his admirable advice-giving on new and sudden occasions; if, as I say, after you have led your artisan to contemplate all these things, you ask him what man this was, no doubt he will readily identify him as one of the fugitives from the battle of Pharsalia: for, to make a judgment about a great commander, it is necessary either to be one or to be capable of becoming one by instruction.[1] It scarcely does an athlete any good to display the strength and vigor of his limbs to some horse with the idea of persuading it that he will take the prize in wrestling, since, for all the horse knows, it might be a contest in hairsplitting. Similarly, enquire of this man what he thinks of Plato and he will fill your ear with praises of a heavenly

---

[1] On the fly-leaf of the copy of Julius Caesar's *Commentarii* that he owned, Montaigne had noted "la grandeur incomparable de cette âme" [the incomparable greatness of that soul]. Cf. Villey, ed., 1274, n. to 416, line 21. The battle of Pharsalia decided the victory of Caesar over Pompey (48 B.C.). Montaigne mentions it eight times in the *Essais*. Montaigne also saw Caesar as deeply flawed, however, in keeping with Marie de Gournay's subsequent reference—see below, 59–61, and n. 48.

mais si vous laissez tomber en ses mains le *Sympose* ou l'*Apologie*[2], il l'en fera des cornets à poivre[3]: et s'il entre en la bouticque d'Apelles[4], il emportera bien son tableau, mais il n'achetera que le nom du peintre[5].

    Ces considerations m'ont tousjours mise en doubte de la valleur des livres et des esprits (je ne parle pas des anciens, de qui nous eslevons la reputation, non par nous, ains par l'authorité des belles ames qui nous ont precedez en leur cognoissance) que le credit populaire suivoit: tant à cause que la fortune et la raison logent rarement ensemble que par ce que je discernois aussi que celuy qui gaignoit multitude d'admirateurs ne pouvoit pas estre grand puisque, pour avoir beaucoup de juges, il faut avoir beaucoup de semblables ou d'approchans au moins. Le vulgaire est une foulle d'aveugles: quiconque se vente de son approbation se vente d'estre honneste homme à qui ne le voit pas. C'est une espece d'injure, d'estre loüé de ceulx que vous ne voudriez pas ressembler. Qu'est-ce donc que le dire de la commune? c'est ce que nulle ame sage ne voudroit ne dire ne croire; la raison? le contrepoil de son opinion. Et trouve la reigle de bien vivre aussi certaine à fuyr l'exemple et le sens du siecle qu'à suivre la Philosophie ou la Theologie. Il ne faut entrer chez le peuple que pour le plaisir d'en sortir. Et peuple et vulgaire s'estend jusques là qu'il est en un estat moins de non vulgaires que de Princes.

    Tu devines ja, Lecteur, que je me veux plaindre du froid recueil, que

---

    [2] Le *Symposium,* aujourd'hui appelé plutôt le *Banquet,* et l'*Apologie de Socrate* sont deux des plus célèbres ouvrages de Platon. Montaigne s'était inspiré du *Banquet* dans les additions à son chapitre «De l'Amitié» (I, 28) et en plusieurs autres endroits (III, 5, 877 C et 884 C; III, 13, 1109 B, C et 1110 B). Les références à Socrate sont très nombreuses dans les *Essais.*

    [3] On vendait le poivre au marché dans des cornets de papier. Montaigne avait employé la même image, espérant que les pages de ses *Essais* puissent au moins servir de papier d'emballage: «J'empescheray peut-estre quelque coin de beurre ne se fonde au marché» (II, 18, 664 C).

    [4] Apelle: le plus illustre peintre de l'Antiquité. Cf. III, 8, 932 B. Marie de Gournay publia une épigramme «Sur la Venus d'Apelles» dans son *Proumenoir de Monsieur de Montaigne* (Paris, Abel L'Angelier, 1594), pp. 74–75.

    [5] Echo ici du début de l'essai «De la Gloire»: «Il y a le nom et la chose [...]» (II, 16, 618 A).

philosopher; but if you let the *Symposium* or the *Apology* fall into his hands,[2] he will make cones for pepper out of it:[3] and if he enters the shop of Apelles,[4] he will indeed come away with his picture, but he will be buying only the name of the painter.[5]

These considerations have always led me to doubt the value of the books and the intellects accorded popular favor (I am not speaking of the ancients, whose reputation we exalt, not on our own, but on the authority of those rare spirits who preceded us in acquaintance with them): as much because fortune and reason rarely dwell together as because I also perceived that he who wins a multitude of admirers could not be great, since, in order to have many judges, there must be many people identical or at least similar. The vulgar are a crowd of the blind: whoever boasts of their approbation boasts of being noble in the sight of those who do not see him. It is a kind of insult to be praised by those you would not wish to resemble. What then is the speech of the common people?—what no wise spirit would wish either to say or to believe; reason?—the opposite of their opinion. And I find the rule of right living as surely in fleeing the example and the judgment of the world as in following philosophy or theology. One should not come amongst the common people except for the pleasure of getting away from them. And the common people and the vulgar extend so far that in any state there are fewer who are not vulgar than there are princes.

You gather already, Reader, that I want to complain about the cold

---

[2] The *Symposium* and the *Apology of Socrates* are two of the most celebrated works of Plato. Montaigne had been inspired by the *Symposium* in the additions to his chapter "De l'amitié [Of Friendship]" (Villey, ed., 1.28.183-195; trans. Florio, 1: 195-209) and in many other places—e.g., Villey, ed., 3.5.877(C) (trans. Florio, 3: 106), 3.13.1109(B,C), and 3.13.1110(B) (trans. Florio, 3: 377-378). References to Socrates are very numerous in the *Essais*.

[3] Pepper was sold in the market in paper cones. Montaigne had employed a similar image, hoping that the pages of his *Essais* might at least serve as wrapping paper: "'j'empescheray peut-estre que quelque coin de beurre ne se fonde au marché [I may peradventure hinder the melting of some piece of butter in the market]" (Villey, ed., 2.18.664[C]; trans. Florio, 2: 391). It is tempting to speculate that, in gratuitously adding the phrase, "or a Grocer from selling an ounce of pepper" (2: 391), which actually reverses the meaning of his original, Florio was recalling Marie de Gournay's comment in the Preface.

[4] Apelles: the most illustrious painter of antiquity. Cf. Villey, ed., 3.8.932(B); trans. Florio, 3: 170. Marie de Gournay published an epigram "Sur la Venus d'Apelles" [On the Venus of Apelles] in *Le Proumenoir de Monsieur de Montaigne* (Paris: Abel L'Angelier, 1594), 74-75. (This is the edition of *Le Proumenoir* referred to in subsequent notes, unless otherwise indicated.)

[5] An echo here of the opening of the essay "De la gloire [On Glory]": "Il y a le nom et la chose … [There is both name, and the thing …]" (Villey, ed., 2.16.618[A]; trans. Florio, 2: 340).

nos hommes ont fait aux *Essais*; et cuydes peult-estre avoir suject d'accuser ma querimonie, en ce que leur ouvrier mesme dit que l'approbation publicque l'encouragea d'amplifier les premiers[6]. Certes, si nous estions de ceux qui croyent que la plus insigne des vertus c'est de se mescognoistre soy-mesme, je te dirois qu'il a pensé, pour gagner la couronne d'humilité, que la renommée de ce livre suffit à son merite; mais parce qu'il n'est rien que nous hayons tant que l'usage de ceste ancienne Lamye[7], aveugle chez elle et clairvoiante ailleurs, d'autant que nous sçavons que qui ne se cognoist bien ne peult bien user de soy-mesme, je te diray que la faveur publique dont il parle n'est pas celle qu'il cuidoit qu'on luy deust, mais bien celle qu'il pensoit tant moins obtenir qu'une plus plaine et plus perfaicte luy estoit mieux deuë[8].

Je rends un sacrifice à la fortune qu'une si fameuse et digne main que celle de Justus Lipsius ayt ouvert les portes de louange aux *Essais*[9]. Et,

---

[6] Montaigne parle de la «faveur publique», c'est-à-dire du succès de son livre, qui lui a donné la «hardiesse» d'écrire davantage (les fameux «allongeails»). Cf. III, 9, 963–964 B. A propos du «recueil», c'est-à-dire de la réception critique de l'édition de 1588, voir Alan M. Boase, *The Fortunes of Montaigne. A History of the «Essais» in France, 1580–1669*, Londres, Methuen, 1935; réédition New York, Octagon Books, 1970, chapitre IV.

[7] La lamie était un être fabuleux qui passait pour dévorer les enfants et qu'on représentait ordinairement avec une tête de femme et un corps de serpent.

[8] Dès l'Avis «Au Lecteur» Montaigne nous dit qu'il n'a «nulle consideration de [sa] gloire» et qu'il n'a pas voulu «rechercher la faveur du monde». *Essais*, éd. cit, p. 3.

[9] Juste Lipse (1547–1606), fameux humaniste flamand, professeur à Iéna, Leyde et Louvain. Il avait écrit à Montaigne en 1588 pour le féliciter. Marie de Gournay correspondra avec lui dès 1589, lui envoyant un échantillon de ses écrits et lui demandant de jouer un rôle semblable à celui de Montaigne vis-à-vis d'elle. Lipse lui répondra par des compliments, la priant de le regarder «comme un frère». C'est de lui qu'elle apprendra la nouvelle de la mort de Montaigne en juin 1593. Cf. Elyane Dezon-Jones, *Fragments d'un discours féminin*, Paris, José Corti, 1988, pp. 24–26 et 186–191. Lipse se ravisa peut-être sur le tard, regrettant d'avoir prodigué son estime trop libéralement à Marie de Gournay. Cf. G. Abel, «Juste Lipse et Marie de Gournay», *Bibliothèque d'Humanisme et Renaissance*, n° 35, 1973, pp. 128–129.

reception that our men[6] have accorded the *Essays*; and perhaps you suppose that you have grounds to condemn my complaining, in that their author himself says that public approval encouraged him to add to the first ones.[7] Certainly, if we were amongst those who believe that the most notable of the virtues is to fail to know oneself,[8] I would tell you that he thought—as was worthy of the crown of humility—that the renown of this book is sufficient to its merit; but because there is nothing we hate so much as the practice of that ancient Lamia,[9] blind in her own house and endowed with sight elsewhere—the more so because we know that someone who does not know himself well cannot make good use of himself—I will tell you that the public favor of which he speaks is not what he believed due to him, but rather what he thought so much less of obtaining that a fuller and more perfect favor was all the more due to him.[10]

I render homage to Fortune that such a famous and worthy hand as that of Justus Lipsius has opened the gates of praise to the *Essays*.[11]

---

[6] Although the expression was common, "nos hommes" anticipates Marie de Gournay's subsequent point that literature in her time and place was a male affair.

[7] Montaigne speaks of the "faveur publique [Publike favor]," that is, the success of his book, which has given him the "hardiesse [boldnes]" to write more—the famous "allongeail[s] [addition(s)]" (Villey, ed., 3.9.963-964[B]; trans. Florio, 3: 205-206). With regard to the critical reception of the edition of 1588, see Alan M. Boase, *The Fortunes of Montaigne: A History of the* Essais *in France, 1580-1669* (1935; repr. New York: Octagon, 1970), chap. 4.

[8] "[S]e mescognoistre soy-mesme" inverts the famous injunction of the Delphic Oracle: "connais-toi toi-même" [know thyself]. For a thorough Renaissance discussion of the maxim in a work undoubtedly known to Marie de Gournay, see Erasmus, *Adages*, 1.6.95 (*Collected Works of Erasmus*, vol. 32, trans. and annotated R. A. B. Mynors [Toronto: University of Toronto Press, 1989], 62-63).

[9] The lamia was a fabulous being that supposedly devoured children and was usually represented with a woman's head and a serpent's body. Marie de Gournay alludes to the myth that Zeus, taking pity on Lamia's sleeplessness, which had been imposed by Hera, granted to her the capacity to remove and replace her eyes at will.

[10] Beginning with the notice "Au Lecteur [. . . to the Reader]," Montaigne tells us that he has *"nulle consideration . . . de [sa] gloire* [no respect or consideration at all . . . to (his) glory]" and that he does not wish to *"rechercher la faveur du monde* [purchase the worlds opinion and favour]" (Villey, ed., 3[A]; trans. Florio, 1: 15).

[11] Justus Lipsius (1547-1606), famous Flemish humanist, professor at Jena, Leyden, and Louvain. He had written to Montaigne in 1588 to congratulate him. Marie de Gournay would correspond with him beginning in 1589, sending him a sample of her writings and asking him to play a role for her similar to that of Montaigne. Lipsius responded with compliments, inviting her to regard him "as a brother." It was from him that she would hear the news of the death of Montaigne in June 1593. Cf. *Fragments d'un discours féminin*, ed. Élyan Dezon-Jones ([Paris]: Corti, 1988), 24-26 and 186-191. Lipsius may later have changed his mind, regretting that he had lavished his esteem too liberally on Marie de Gournay. Cf. Günter Abel, "Juste Lipse et Marie de Gournay autour de *l'exemplaire d'Anvers* des *Essais de Montaigne*," *Bibliothèque d'Humanisme et Renaissance* 35 (1973): 128-129.

en ce qu'elle l'a choisy pour en parler le premier, elle a voulu luy defferer une prerogative de suffisance et nous advertir tous de l'escouter comme nostre maistre. On estoit prest à me donner de l'hellebore lors que, comme ils me furent fortuitement mis en main au sortir de l'enfance[10], ils me transsissoient d'admiration, si je ne me fusse à propos targuée de l'eloge que ce personnage leur avoit rendu dez quelques annees, m'estant monstré lors que je vis premierement leur auteur mesme, que ce m'est tant de gloire d'appeller Pere, apres qu'ils m'eurent fait souhaitter deux ans cette sienne rencontre, avec la vehemente solicitude que plusieurs ont cognue, et nul sans crier miracle[11]. *Platinus nunc adest* (dit Lipsius en l'epistre 43 *Centurie I*) *seriò à me, monitus de Thalete illo Gallico, etc.* Et puis: *Apud nos scilicet sapientia illa non habitat*. Et en la marge se lit: *Ita indigetavi probum, sapientem librum Michaëlis Montani.* En l'epistre 45 *Centurie II* qu'il escrit à luy-mesme: *Non, blandiamur*

---

[10] Dans la *Copie de la Vie de la Damoiselle de Gournay* (1616) on lit: «Environ les dix-huit ou dix-neuf ans [c'est-à-dire vers 1584], cette fille lut les *Essais* par hasard; et bien qu'ils fussent nouveaux encore et sans nulle reputation qui pust guider son jugement, elle les mit non seulement à leur juste prix, trait fort difficile à faire en tel aage, et en un siecle si peu suspect de porter de tels fruits, mais elle commença de desirer la connaissance de leur auteur, plus que toutes les choses du monde.» Ed. Dezon-Jones, p. 138.

[11] C'est au printemps de 1588 que Marie de Gournay rencontra Montaigne, pour la première fois, à Paris. Il s'était donc écoulé quatre, et non deux ans, depuis la lecture des *Essais*.

And, given that Fortune chose him to be the first to speak about them, she wished to accord him the prerogative of sufficiency[12] and warn us all to listen to him as our master. They were ready to give me hellebore,[13] sent into ecstasy as I was when the *Essays* were fortuitously put into my hands at the point when I was leaving childhood behind,[14] if I had not propitiously shielded myself with the encomium which that worthy man had rendered them some years earlier. That praise proved to be justified,[15] when, after the *Essays* had made me long to meet him for two years, I first saw the author of the *Essays* himself, whom I am so honored in calling Father, display the eager solicitude that—no surprise—many have experienced.[16] *Plantinus nunc adest* (says Lipsius in letter 43, *Century I*) *serió à me, monitus de Thalete illo Gallico, etc.* And later: *Apud nos scilicet sapientia illa non habitat.* And in the margin is found: *Ita indigetavi probum, sapientem librum Michaëlis Montani.* In letter 45, *Century II*, which he writes to Montaigne himself:

---

[12] The obsolete commendatory senses of "suffisant" and "suffisance" translate poorly into modern English ("capable" and "capability," not to mention "wise" and "wisdom," make feeble approximations), so it has seemed preferable to use the literal equivalents, which were current in Elizabethan English (including Florio's) with similar connotations. It is worth noting that Marie de Gournay sometimes, in revisions undertaken toward the mid-seventeenth century, substituted "doctrine" or "sapience" for "suffisance" (thus in the 1634 and 1641 editions of *Égalité des hommes et des femmes*, first published in 1622). Certainly, for her, as for Renaissance Humanists generally, learning—and the moral development understood to follow from it—formed an essential part of the ideal of "sufficiency" (cf. below, 59–65).

[13] As a treatment for madness—a standard remedy since antiquity (see Pliny, the Elder, *Natural History*, vol. 7, ed. and trans. W. H. S. Jones, Loeb Classical Library [London: Heinemann; Cambridge, MA: Harvard University Press, 1956], 180–181 [25.60]). Cf. Erasmus, *Adages*, 1.8.51 (*Collected Works*, 32: 152–153).

[14] In the *Copie de la vie de la damoiselle de Gournay* (1616), one reads:

Environ les dix-huit ou dix-neuf ans, cette fille lut les *Essais* par hasard: et bien qu'ils fussent nouveaux encore et sans nulle réputation qui pût guider son jugement, elle les mit non seulement à leur juste prix, trait fort difficile à faire en tel âge, et en un siècle si peu suspect de porter de tels fruits, mais elle commença de désirer la connaissance de leur auteur, plus que toutes les choses du monde.

[At about eighteen or nineteen years of age (that is, around 1584), that girl read the *Essays* by chance; and although they were still recent and without any reputation which might guide her judgment, not only did she rate them at their true value, something difficult indeed to do at such an age, and in an era so little suspected of bearing such fruit, but she began to desire acquaintance with their author more than anything in the world.]   (Dezon-Jones, ed., *Discours féminin*, 138)

[15] The antecedent of "m'estant monstré" remains ambiguous in the long and tangled original sentence (here divided into two for the sake of clarity).

[16] It was in the spring of 1588, in Paris, that Marie de Gournay met Montaigne for the first time. Four years, therefore, and not two, had elapsed since her reading of the *Essais*.

inter nos, ego te talem censeo, qualem publicè descripsi uno verbo. Inter septem illos te referam, aut si quid sapientius illis septem[12]. C'est parler cela Lipsius, et les *Essais* estoyent esgallement capables, qui d'impartir, qui de meriter l'extreme honneur. C'est de telles ames qu'il fault souhaitter la ressemblance et la bonne opinion.

Quel malheur n'a voulu que je te puisse aussi produire les lettres, que le sieur d'Ossat luy escrivit sur le mesme sujet[13]? Homme, pour la recommandation duquel, à ceux qui ne cognoissent pas son prix, il suffit de dire que c'estoit la personne d'Italie où ce Gascon reside, plus aymée et plus estimée de mon Pere; et ne puis, Lecteur, l'appeller autrement; car je ne suis moy-mesme que par où je suis sa fille. Si n'a il point tenu à la diligente recherche de madame de Montaigne[14], qu'elle ne les ait trouvées parmy les papiers du deffunct, quand elle m'envoya ces derniers escripts pour les mettre au jour. Elle a tout son pays pour tesmoing d'avoir rendu les offices d'une tres-ardente amour conjugale à la memoire de son mary, sans espargner travaux ny despence; mais je puis tesmoigner en verité, pour le particulier de ce livre, que son maistre mesme n'en eust jamais eu tant de soing, et plus considerable, de ce qu'il se r'encontroit en saison, en laquelle la langueur, où les pleurs et les douleurs de sa perte l'avoient precipitée, l'en eust peu justement et decemment dispenser. Qualifierons nous ces larmes odieuses ou desirables? veu que, si Dieu l'a reservée au plus lamentable des veufvages, il luy a pour le moins assigné quand et quand en luy le plus honnorable tiltre qui soit entre les femmes? Et n'est Dame de merite et de valeur, qui n'aymast mieux avoir eu son mary, qu'en avoir nul autre, tel qu'il

---

[12] Lettre à Théodore Leeuw (1583): «[Christophe] Plantin [le celèbre imprimeur d'Anvers] est maintenant au courant; je lui ai recommandé sérieusement ce Thalès français. [...] Il est clair qu'une telle sagesse n'existe pas parmi nous. [...] En fait, je lui ai signalé [à Plantin] ce livre honnête et sage de Michel de Montaigne.» Juste Lipse, *Epistolarum Centuria* I, lettre 43, Anvers, 1591, p. 69. Lettre à Montaigne (1588): «N'usons pas de flatterie entre nous: je t'estime tel que je t'ai décrit publiquement en quelques mots. Je te placerai parmi ces Sept [Sages de la Grèce], voire même—si c'est possible—plus sage qu'eux sept.» Ibid., II, lettre 45, p. 52.

[13] Arnaud d'Ossat (1536-1604), gascon comme Montaigne, secrétaire de Paul de Foix à Rome, négocia l'abjuration d'Henri IV. Montaigne raconte qu'il s'était promené avec lui à Rome (*Journal de Voyage*, éd. Fausta Garavini, Paris, Gallimard, 1983, p. 254). C'est en lui écrivant que l'auteur des *Essais* s'était soudain souvenu de La Boétie, dix-sept ans après la mort de ce dernier (Ibid., p. 277).

[14] Madame de Montaigne: Françoise de la Chassaigne que Montaigne avait épousé en 1565. Marie de Gournay fait son éloge à la fin de la Préface et lui dédie un quatrain à la fin du *Proumenoir* (p. 76).

Non, blandiamur inter nos, ego te talem censeo, qualem publicè descripsi uno verbo. Inter septem illos te referam, aut si quid sapientius illis septem.[17] That is how Lipsius speaks, and the *Essays* were a match for him—he imparting, they deserving, the greatest honor. It is such spirits who should be emulated and whose good opinion should be wished.

What unhappy chance willed it that I cannot also produce for you the letters that Lord Ossat wrote to him on the same subject?[18] It is a sufficient recommendation of this man, for those unacquainted with his worth, to say that he was the person in Italy (where that native of Gascony resides) best loved and esteemed by my Father—and I cannot, Reader, use another name for him, for I am not myself except insofar as I am his daughter. It is scarcely a reflection on the diligent search made by Madame de Montaigne[19] that she had not found the letters amongst his papers after his death, when she sent me these last writings to publish. She has all her country to witness that she has rendered all the offices of an ardent conjugal love to the memory of her husband, sparing neither trouble nor expense; but I can truthfully attest, with specific regard to this book, that her lord himself would never have taken such pains, and these were the greater because they came at a time when she would justly and properly have been excused, given the exhaustion into which she was plunged by the weeping and suffering occasioned by her loss. Shall we account those tears hateful or desirable, seeing that, if God has destined her for the most miserable of widowhoods, He has at least concurrently conferred upon her the most honorable title that a woman may hold? And there is no lady of merit and worth who would not rather have had her husband than have any other, whoever he might be.

---

[17] Letter to Theodore Leeuw (1583): "[Christophe] Plantin [the famous printer from Antwerp] is now with us, having been earnestly informed by me about that Gallic Thales. [...] Amongst us, certainly, there dwells no such wisdom. [...] Thus I have invoked the virtuous, wise book of Michel de Montaigne" (Justus Lipsius, *Justi Lipsii Epistolarum centuriae duae, etc.*, 2 vols. in 1 [Antwerp: C. Plantin, 1591], 1.43 [p. 69]). Letter to Montaigne (1588): "Let us not flatter between ourselves; I judge you to be such as I publicly described you in a single word. I shall set you down amongst those Seven [Sages of Greece], or above them, if anything may be wiser" (2.45 [p. 52]).

[18] Arnaud d'Ossat (1536–1604), a Gascon like Montaigne, the secretary of Paul de Foix at Rome, negotiated the abjuration of Henri IV. Montaigne relates that he had gone round with him in Rome (*Journal de voyage*, ed. Fausta Garavini [Paris: Gallimard, 1983], 254). It was in writing to him that the author of the *Essais* had suddenly recalled the death of La Boétie, seventeen years after the latter's death (*Journal*, 277).

[19] Madame de Montaigne: Françoise de la Chassaigne, whom Montaigne had married in 1565. Marie de Gournay pays tribute to her at the end of the Preface and dedicates a quatrain to her at the end of *Le Proumenoir* (76).

soit. Haut et glorieux advantage que le pis, dont Dieu l'ait estimée digne, reste encore achetable au prix de toute autre felicité. Chaqu'un luy doibt, sinon autant de graces, au moins autant de louanges que je faiz: d'avoir voulu r'embrasser et r'échauffer en moy les cendres de son mary, et non pas l'espouser mais se rendre une autre luy-mesme, ressuscitant en elle à son trespas une affection où jamais elle n'avoit participé que par les oreilles, voire luy restituer un nouvel image de vie par la continuation de l'amitié qu'il me portoit.

Les *Essais* m'ont tousjours servy de touche pour esprouver les esprits, requerant mille et mille de me donner instruction de ce que j'en devois estimer, afin de m'instruire, selon le degré du bien qu'ils en jugeroient, le bien que je debvois juger d'eux-mesmes. Le jugement est l'office de tous auquel les hommes s'applicquent de plus diverse mesure: le plus rare present que Dieu leur face, leur perfection[15]. Tous biens, ouy les essenciels, leur sont inutiles si cestuy-là ne les mesnage, et la vertu mesme tient sa forme de luy. Le seul jugement esleve les humains sur les bestes, Socrates sur eux, Dieu sur luy. Le seul jugement nous met en

---

[15] Eloge du «jugement» qui fait écho à ce qu'en dit Montaigne. Voir, par exemple, I, 26, 152 A.

It is a great and glorious benefit that the worst of which God has judged her to be worthy still rates at the value of all other happiness. Everyone owes her, if not so much gratitude, at least as much praise as I accord her for having wished to rekindle and rewarm in me the ashes of her husband, and, not to marry him, but to make of herself another him—reviving in herself at his death an affection in which she had never participated except by hearing of it—and so truly to restore to him a new appearance of life by the continuation of the friendship that he bore me.

The *Essays* have always served me as a touchstone for testing intellects, and I have asked person after person to instruct me as to what I should think of them, so that I might be instructed, according to what degree of worth others saw in them, as to what worth I should see in others. Judgment is the one of all the functions to which men apply themselves in the most diverse measures—the rarest gift that God bestows on them, their perfection.[20] All good qualities, yea the essential ones, are useless to them unless that one controls them, and virtue itself derives its form from it. Judgment alone raises human beings above the beasts, Socrates above them, God above him. Judgment

---

[20] A tribute to judgment ("jugement") that echoes what Montaigne says of it. See, e.g., Villey, ed., 1.25.136(A) (trans. Florio, 1: 138) and 1.26.152(A) (trans. Florio, 1: 157); in both instances, the term is closely allied with understanding ("entendement"). As the eminence accorded Socrates in Marie de Gournay's discussion indicates, her exaltation of judgment throughout the Preface is heavily Platonic; cf. R. C. Lodge, *Plato's Theory of Ethics: The Moral Criterion and the Highest Good* (London: Kegan Paul; New York: Harcourt, 1928), esp. 7–173.

droicte possession de Dieu: cela s'appelle l'adorer, et l'ignorer.

Vous plaist il avoir l'esbat de veoir eschauder plaisamment les Censeurs des *Essais?* Mettez les sur les livres anciens; je ne dis pas pour

alone puts us in true possession of God: this is called adoring Him, and not knowing Him.[21]

Would you like to have the pleasure of seeing the Censors of the

---

[21] The wording ("l'adorer, et l'ignorer") marks an allusion to the skeptically grounded principle that true judgment in divine matters means worshiping God without presuming to know Him—a virtual summary of Montaigne's Christianized Pyrrhonism in "Apologie de Raimond Sebond [An Apologie of *Raymond Sebond*]": "La peste de l'homme, c'est l'opinion de sçavoir. Voylà pourquoy l'ignorance nous est tant recommandée par nostre religion comme piece propre à la creance et à l'obeïssance [*The opinion of wisdome is the plague of man*. That is the occasion why ignorance is by our Religion recommended unto us, as an instrument fitting beleefe, and obedience]" (Villey, ed., 2.12.488[A]; trans. Florio, 2: 186). The point is anticipated in "C'est folie de rapporter le vray et le faux a nostre suffisence [It Is Folly to Referre Truth or Falshood to Our Sufficiencie]":

> ... la raison m'a instruit que de condamner ainsi resoluement une chose pour fauce et impossible, c'est se donner l'advantage d'avoir dans la teste les bornes et limites de la volonté de Dieu et de la puissance de nostre mere nature; et qu'il n'y a point de plus notable folie au monde que de les ramener à la mesure de nostre capacité et suffisance.

> [... reason hath taught me, that so resolutely to condemne a thing for false, and impossible, is to assume unto himselfe the advantage, to have the bounds and limits of Gods will, and of the power of our common mother Nature tied to his sleeve: And that there is no greater folly in the world, than to reduce them to the measure of our capacitie, and bounds of our sufficiencie.]
> (Villey, ed., 1.27.179[A]; trans. Florio, 1: 191)

Cf. Marie de Gournay below, 55–57: "Who, moreover, could tolerate those heaven-climbing Titans that think to arrive at God by their own means and circumscribe His works by the limits of their reason? Instead, we say that precisely where things are more incredible they are more certainly the workings of God, and that God is neither here nor there if there is no miracle." One wonders whether, in her juxtaposition of "adorer" and "ignorer," Marie de Gournay particularly recalled (from the "Apologie"), "Les choses les plus ignorées sont plus propres à estre deifiées [Things most unknowne are fittest to bee deified]" (Villey, ed., 2.12.516[A]; trans. Florio, 2: 220), given that hers was the first edition to omit the phrase that follows, which begins, "car d'adorer celles de nostre sorte, maladifves, corruptibles et mortelles, comme faisoit toute l'ancienneté ... " [for to adore those sickly, corruptible, and mortal things belonging to our species, as they did in all ancient times ...] (Villey, ed., 2.12.516 n. 11). (Florio's use of the edition of 1595 or 1598 is thereby confirmed.)

That her stark and cryptic language lent itself to misconstruction is suggested by the clarifying revisions offered by later versions of the Preface, beginning in 1599 with "cela s'appelle l'ignorer et l'adorer" [this is called not knowing Him and adoring Him] ("Préface de 1599," ed. Anna Lia Franchetti, *Montaigne Studies* 8.1-2 [1996]: 181), and changing in 1617 to "Cela s'apelle ignorer & l'adorer en la foy" [This is called not knowing and adoring him in faith] ("Preface to the 1617 Edition," ed. Mary McKinley, *Montaigne Studies* 8.1-2 [1996]: 205). On this point, cf. Franchetti, ed., 181 n. 11; Marjorie Henry Ilsley, *A Daughter of the Renaissance: Marie le Jars de Gournay: Her Life and Works* (The Hague: Mouton, 1963), 69; and Boase, who compares Pierre Charron, *Trois vérités*, 1.5 ("La vraie connaissance de Dieu est une parfaite ignorance de lui" [cited Boase, *Fortunes of Montaigne*, 59 n. 3]), and insists (72)—excessively, perhaps—on Marie de Gournay's "complete" separation of the spheres of reason and faith. On these aspects of the thought of Montaigne and Charron in the contemporary theological context, see Don Cameron Allen, *Doubt's Boundless Sea: Skepticism and Faith in the Renaissance* (Baltimore, MD: The Johns Hopkins Press, 1964), 75–97; cf. Hiram Haydn, *The Counter-Renaissance* (New York: Harcourt, 1950), 76–130.

leur demander si Plutarque et Seneque sont de grands autheurs car la reputation, les dresse en ce point là, mais pour sçavoir de quelle part ils le sont plus: si c'est au jugement, si c'est en l'esprit; qui frappe plus ferme en tel et tel endroict; quelle a deu estre leur fin en escrivant; quelle des fins d'escrire est la meilleure; quelle de leurs pieces ils pourroient perdre avec moins d'interest; quelle ils devroient garder avant toutes, et pourquoy. Fay leur apres espelucher une comparaison de l'utilité de leur doctrine contre celle d'autres escrivains, et finablement trier ceux de tous qu'ils aymeroient mieux ressembler et dissembler. Quiconque sçaura pertinemment respondre de cela, je luy donne loy de corriger ma creance des *Essais*.

Bien heureux es tu, Lecteur, si tu n'ez pas d'un sexe qu'on ait interdit de tous les biens, l'interdisant de la liberté, et encores interdit de toutes les vertus, luy soubstrayant le pouvoir en la moderation de l'usage duquel elles se forment: affin de luy constituer pour vertu seulle et beatitude, ignorer et souffrir. Bien heureux, qui peuz estre sage sans crime, le sexe te concedant toute action et parolle juste, et le credit d'en estre creu, ou pour le moins escouté. De moy, veux-je mettre mes gens à cet examen où il y a des cordes que les doigts feminins ne doibvent, dit-on, toucher; ou bien, eussé-je les argumens de Carneades[16], il n'y a si chetif qui ne me r'embarre, avec solenne approbation de la compagnie assistante, par un soubsris, un hochet ou quelque plaisanterie, quand il aura dit: «C'est une femme qui parle»[17].

---

[16] Carnéade de Cyrène: philosophe, fondateur de la troisième Académie. Montaigne le cite en exemple une dizaine de fois dans les *Essais*.
[17] Tout ce passage sera repris, corrigé (suppression des répétitions) et amplifié dans le texte intitulé «Grief des Dames», publié dans *L'Ombre de la Demoiselle de Gournay*, Paris, Jean Libert, 1626. Cf. Dezon-Jones, pp. 129-133.

Essays amusingly stewed in their own juice? Put them on to the ancient books—not, I mean, in order to ask them if Plutarch and Seneca are great authors, for reputation will set them straight on that point, but in order to know in what quality that greatness chiefly consists: whether it lies in judgment or intellect; who is more striking in such and such a passage; what their aims must have been in writing; which of their aims in writing carries more weight; which one of their works might be dispensed with at the least cost; which should be preserved above all, and why. Then have our Censors work out a comparison between these writers and others with regard to the usefulness of their teaching, and, finally, have them sort out from all writers those whom they would most wish to be like, and to differ from. Whoever will know how to respond fitly on these points—to him I grant the right to correct my opinion of the *Essays*.

Blessed indeed are you,[22] Reader, if you are not of a sex that has been forbidden all possessions, is forbidden liberty, has even been forbidden all the virtues, being denied the power (from which these are formed) of exercising moderation in experience—all for the sake of establishing, as its sole virtue and happiness, ignorance and suffering. Blessed indeed are you, who can be wise without committing a crime, since your sex accords you the privilege of every proper action and speech, as well as the favor to have what you say believed, or at least listened to. As for me, if I wish to put my auditors to the sort of examination that involves, it is said, strings that female fingers cannot touch, even had I the arguments of Carneades,[23] there is no one so much a weakling that he will not rebuke me, to the grave approbation of the company present, with a smile, a nod, or some jest, which will have the effect of saying, "It's a woman speaking."[24]

---

[22] Our translation reflects the likelihood that, in her repeated use of "Bien heureux," Marie de Gournay is ironically adapting the formula familiar from the Beatitudes: "Bien-heureux sont ..." (*La saincte Bible ... Traduicte de Latin en François par les Théologiens de l'Université de Louvain, etc.* [1572; Lyon: Thibaud Ancelin, 1603], Matt. 5:3ff.); "Vous estes bien-heureux vous ..." (Luke 6:20); "Vous serez bien-heureux ..." (Luke 6:22).

[23] Carneades of Cyrene: philosopher, founder of the third Academy. Montaigne cites him as an example some ten times in the *Essais*.

[24] The whole of this passage would be used again, revised (to eliminate repetitions) and amplified, in the text entitled *Grief des dames*, published in *L'Ombre de la demoiselle de Gournay* (Paris: Jean Libert, 1626) and reprinted in Dezon-Jones, ed., *Discours féminin*, 129–133. See also the Notice to the edition of Constant Venesoen, *Égalité des hommes et des femmes, Grief des dames, Le Proumenoir de Monsieur de Montaigne*, by Marie de Gournay (Geneva: Droz, 1993), 59–62.

Tel, se taisant par mespris, ravira le monde en admiration de sa gravité, qu'il raviroit d'autre sorte, à l'adventure, si vous l'obligiez de mettre un peu par escript ce qu'il eust voulu respondre aux propositions et repliques de ceste femelle s'elle eust esté masle. Un autre, arresté de sa foiblesse à my-chemin, souz couleur de ne vouloir pas importuner son adversaire, sera dit victorieux et courtois ensemble. Cetuy-là, disant trente sottises, emportera le prix encore par sa barbe. Cestuy-cy sera frappé, qui n'a pas l'entendement de le sentir, d'une main de femme; et tel autre le sent, qui tourne le discours en risée ou bien en escopterie de caquet perpetuel, sans donner place aux responces; ou il le tourne ailleurs et se met à vomir plaisamment force belles choses qu'on ne luy demande pas. Luy, qui sçait combien il est aysé de faire son prouffit des oreilles de l'assistance, qui pour se trouver tres-rarement capable de juger de l'ordre et conduitte de la dispute, et de la force des combatans, ou de ne s'esblouyr pas à l'esclat de ceste vaine science qu'il crache (comme s'il estoit question de rendre compte de sa leçon et non pas de respondre) ne peult s'appercevoir quand ces gallanteries là sont fuitte ou victoire. Cet autre, en fin, bravant une femme, fera cuider à sa grand'mere que, s'il n'estoit pitoyable, Hercules ne vivroit pas[18]. Heureux à qui, pour emporter le prix, il ne faille que fuir les coups, et qui puisse acquerir autant de gloire qu'il veult espargner de labeur. Bravant dis-je, une femme offusquée et atterrée en outre, d'une profonde tardiveté d'entendement et d'invention, d'une memoire si tendre que trois raisons d'un adversaire qu'elle voudroit retenir en disputant l'accablent, de la simplicité de sa condition, et sur tout d'un visage le plus ridiculement mol du monde. Je veux un mal si horrible à cette imperfection, qui me blesse tant, qu'il faut que je l'injurie en public. Je pardonne à ceux qui s'en mocquent: se sont-ils obligez d'estre aussi habiles qu'Aristippus ou Xenophon pour aller discerner souz un visage qui

---

[18] «De plus, elles [les femmes] ont plusieurs fois emporté et arboré [de hautes victoires] en divers climats du Monde; mais sur quelles gens encore? Cyrus et Thésée; à ces deux, on ajoute Hercule qu'elles ont sinon vaincu, du moins bien battu.» *Egalité des Hommes et des Femmes* (1622), éd. Dezon-Jones, p. 122. Allusion à l'épisode des Amazones et d'Omphale dans la légende d'Hercule. Sur les Amazones, voir Montaigne, III. 5, 885 C et III, 11, 1033 B.

A certain one, remaining silent out of contempt, will astonish the crowd with his gravity, when he might astonish them otherwise, perhaps, if you obliged him to write down a little of what he would like to have said in response to the poor woman, if she had been a man. Another, stymied half-way by his own feebleness on the pretense of not wishing to embarrass his adversary, will be termed at once victorious and courteous. That fellow there, uttering thirty idiocies, will still take the prize by his beard. This one here, who lacks the understanding to realize it, will be struck by a woman's hand; and someone else *will* realize it and turn the conversation into mockery, or rather into a barrage of incessant cackling with no room for responses; or he turns it elsewhere and amusingly starts to vomit lots of pretty things that he has not been asked for. He knows how easy it is to get the ear of his listeners, who, so that they may regard themselves as exceptional judges of the order and conduct of the debate and the strength of the combatants, or so as not to be dazzled by the explosion of empty learning that he spews (as if it were a matter of reciting his lesson rather than responding), are unable to discern whether those glib phrases amount to a rout or a victorious charge. This other, finally, boldly challenging a woman, will make his grandmother believe that, if he did not take pity, Hercules would not get away from him with his life.[25] (He is a happy man who, to gain the prize, need only flee the blows, and who may acquire as much glory as he wishes to spare pains.) Challenging, I say, a woman benighted and in consternation to boot, of a profound slowness of understanding and invention, with so tender a memory as to be overwhelmed by three points of an adversary that she would like to retain for the argument, who possesses the simplicity of her condition and, above all, the most ridiculously soft countenance in the world. I wish so ill to that imperfection, which does me so much harm, that it behooves me to disparage it in public. I forgive those who make fun of it: need they be as proficient as Aristippus or Xenophon to discern beneath a

---

[25] In *Égalité des hommes et des femmes* (1622), after speaking of the "hautes victoires" [great victories] over powerful men that women "ont plusieurs fois emportées et arborées en divers Climats du Monde" [have several times won and flaunted in various regions of the world], Marie de Gournay continues with an allusion to the episodes of the Amazons and of Omphale in the legend of Hercules: "on ajoute Hercule, qu'elles ont sinon vaincu du moins bien battu" [one may add Hercules, whom they have, if not conquered, at least well beaten] (Dezon-Jones, ed., *Discours féminin*, 122). On the Amazons, see Villey, ed., 3.5.885(C) and 3.11.1033(B) (trans. Florio, 3: 114–115 and 3: 287).

rougit autre chose qu'un esprit sot ou vaincu[19]? Et si leur pardonne encore de penser que telles confessions que cecy partent de folie; il est bien vray qu'elles sont esgalement communes aux fols et aux sages, mais aux sages de tel degré que je ne puis aller jusques là.

Pour venir à nos *Essais*, quant aux reproches particuliers qu'on leur fait, je ne les daignerois r'abatre, afin de les remettre en grace avec les calomniateurs; mais j'en veux dire un mot en faveur de quelques esprits qui meritent bien qu'on employe un advertissement pour les garder de chopper apres eux. Premierement, ils reprennent au langage quelque usurpation du Latin et la fabricque de nouveaux mots; je responds que je leur donne gaigné s'ils peuvent dire pere, ny mere, frere, soeur, boire, manger, veiller, dormir, aller, veoir, sentir, ouyr, et toucher, ny tout le reste en somme des plus communs vocables qui tombent en nostre usage, sans parler Latin. Ouy, mais le besoin d'exprimer nos conceptions nous contraint à l'emprunt de ceulx là; et le besoin de ce personnage, tout de mesme, l'a contraint d'emprunter outre toy ceux-cy, pour exprimer ses conceptions qui sont outre les tiennes. Je sçay bien qu'on a rendu les plus excellens livres en nostre langue, où les traducteurs se sont rendus plus superstitieux d'innover et puiser aux sources estrangeres. Mais on ne dit pas aussi que les *Essais* resserrent en une ligne ce

---

[19] Aristippe de Cyrène (IVe siècle av. J.-C.), philosophe célèbre pour sa «contrefinesse» (I, 26, 171 C). Marie de Gournay avait dû lire Diogène Laërce à son sujet car, dans ses éditions des *Essais,* elle identifiera Aristippe là où Montaigne n'avait pas donné de précisions. C'est le cas justement dans l'essai «De l'Amitié», qu'elle a beaucoup pratiqué, au moment où Montaigne parle du lien naturel qui unit un père à ses enfants (I, 28, 185 C). L'allusion au visage qui rougit et au commentaire d'Aristippe se trouve en III, 5, 884 C. Quant à Xénophon, il écrivit contre la volupté telle que la préconisait Aristippe (III, 9, 989 C).

face that blushes anything but a mind foolish or cowed?[26] Still, I pardon them likewise for thinking that such confessions as these stem from folly; it is true that they are equally to be encountered amongst fools and the wise, but the latter must be wise to a degree that I cannot attain to.

To come to our *Essays*: the particular reproaches directed against them I would not deign to refute in order to restore them to favor with the slanderers; but I wish to say a word on the subject for the sake of certain minds who well deserve a warning to keep them from stumbling after. In the first place, they take the language to task for a kind of usurpation of Latin and coinage of new words; I respond by yielding them the point, if they can say father or mother, brother, sister, drink, eat, wake, sleep, go, see, smell, hear, and touch—or, in sum, all the rest of the most common words it falls to us to use—without speaking Latin. Yes, but the need to express our conceptions compels us to borrow these; and in just the same way, the need of that luminary compelled him to borrow to a greater extent than you in order to express his conceptions, which exceed your own. I am well aware that most excellent books have been rendered into our language, in which the translators took it upon themselves to be more scrupulous about innovating and drawing on foreign sources. But what is not also said is that the *Essays*

---

[26] Aristippus of Cyrene (fourth century B.C.), philosopher celebrated for his "contrefinesse [counter-craft]" (Villey, ed., 1.26.171[C]; trans. Florio, 1: 182) or humorous retort at the expense of oversubtle logic. Marie de Gournay must have read Diogenes Laertius' account of him—she had, after all, translated that author's *Life of Socrates* from the Greek—for, in her editions of the *Essais*, she will identify Aristippus in places where Montaigne had not specified him. As Florio's translation witnesses, this is what occurs in the essay "De l'amitié [Of Friendship]," which she was well acquainted with, at the point where Montaigne speaks of the natural bond that joins a father to his children (Villey, ed., 1.28.185[C]; trans. Florio, 1: 197). The allusion to the face that blushes and the comment of Aristippus may be found in Villey, ed., 3.5.884(C) (trans. Florio, 3: 114) and has reference to the blush of some young men at his entering a brothel. As for Xenophon, he wrote against pleasure such as was advocated by Aristippus: "En toutes les chambrées de la philosophie ancienne cecy se trouvera, qu'un mesme ouvrier y publie des reigles de temperance et publie ensemble des escris d'amour et desbauche. Et Xenophon, au giron de Clinias, escrivit contre la volupté Aristippique [In all the parts of ancient Philosophie, this one thing may be noted, that one same worke-man publisheth some rules of temperance, and there-withall some compositions of love and licentiousnesse. And *Xenophon* in *Cliniaes* bosome, writ against the Aristippian vertue]" (Villey, ed., 3.9.989[B,C]; trans. Florio, 3: 238). Florio's translation is at least elliptical here. For her part, Marie de Gournay, in coupling these two followers of Socrates as "habiles" [proficient], is pointedly uniting opposites and antagonists: "Xenophon was no friend to Aristippus" (Diogenes Laertius, *Lives of Eminent Philosophers*, ed. and trans. R. D. Hicks, Loeb Classical Library [London: Heinemann; New York: Putnam's, 1925], 1: 195 [chap. 8]).

qu'ils trainent en quatre; ny que nous ne sommes point assez sçavans, ny moy ny ceux à l'adventure qui devisent ainsi, pour sentir si leur traduction est par tout aussi roide que leur autheur. J'ayme à dire: «gladiateur», j'ayme à dire: «escrimeur à outrance»; aussi faict ce livre; mais qui m'astreindroit à quitter l'un des deux, je retiendrois pour la brieveté, «gladiateur»; et si sçay bien quel bruit on en menera: par tout en chose semblable je ferois de mesme.

Je sçay bien qu'il faut user de bride aux innovations et aux emprunts; mais n'est ce pas une grand'sottise de dire que si l'on ne deffend autre chose que d'y proceder sans regle, on le prohibe aux *Essais* apres l'avoir permis au *Romant de la rose,* veu mesme que son siecle n'estoit pressé, non plus que le nostre, sinon de la seule necessité d'amendement? car avant ce vieil livre[20] on ne laissoit pas de parler et se faire entendre autant qu'on vouloit. Où la force d'esprit manque, les motz ne manquent jamais. Et suis en doubte, au rebours, qu'en cette large et profonde uberté de la langue Grecque ils ne manquassent encore souvent à Socrates et à Platon. On ne peut representer que les conceptions communes par les mots communs. Quiconque en a d'extraordinaires doit chercher des termes à s'exprimer. C'est, au reste, l'impropre innovation qu'il faut blasmer et non l'innovation aux choses qu'on peut rendre meilleures[21]. Ces gens icy sont plaisans de syndiquer l'innovation absolüement en l'idiome François, parce qu'Æschynes et Calvus[22] l'eussent condemnée aux leurs, sans considerer qu'une qualité contraire, sçavoir est imperfection à cestuy-là, perfection à ceux-cy, rend l'accession esgalement bien à luy et mal à eux. C'est faire comme le singe qui s'enfuiroit bel erre, de peur qu'on ne le prist par la queue, s'il avoit ouy dire qu'un renard auroit esté happé par là.

---

[20] Le texte original porte «ivre» au lieu de «livre», c'est-à-dire le *Roman de la Rose.*

[21] Ce passage très érasmien sur l'importance des choses (*res*) par rapport aux mots (*verba*) est un écho du chapitre «De l'Institution des enfans» (I, 26, en particulier pp. 168–174).

[22] Aeschynes et Calvus: deux célèbres orateurs de l'Antiquité; le premier, rival de Démosthène, et le second, de Cicéron.

compress into one line what the other works drag out over four; or that we are hardly sufficiently learned—neither myself nor perhaps those who speak so—to be aware whether their translation is everywhere as straightforward as their author. I like to say, "gladiator"; I like to say, "swordsman who fights to the finish"—that is how this book is made. But if someone should force me to give up one of the two, I would retain "gladiator" for brevity's sake; and yet I well know what commotion would arise. I would do the same thing everywhere in a similar case.

I well know that restraint must be applied to innovations and borrowings; yet if nothing is prohibited but to innovate and borrow indiscriminately, is it not a great folly to say that the *Essays* are forbidden what has been allowed to *The Romance of the Rose*, especially considering that the era of the latter was under no constraint, any more than ours is, except that of the same need to make improvements? For prior to that ancient book,[27] people did not hold themselves back from speaking and making themselves heard as much as they pleased. Where strength of mind is lacking, words never are. And I remain in doubt, on the other hand, whether in that broad and deep fecundity of the Greek language, words did not often fail Socrates and Plato. With common words, one can represent only common ideas. Whoever has extraordinary ones must search for terms with which to express himself. Moreover, it is improper innovation that ought to be condemned, not innovation in things that may be made better.[28] These people are content absolutely to censure innovation in French expression because Aeschines and Calvus[29] would have had it forbidden to their countrymen, without considering that the contrary circumstances—namely, imperfection on one side, perfection on the other—renders conformity to that stricture equally good in one case and bad in the other. This is to behave like the ape who would make haste to flee, fearing lest he be taken by the tail, if he should hear that a fox had been caught in the same place.

---

[27] The original text reads "ivre" [drunk] in place of "livre" [book], that is, *The Romance of the Rose*.

[28] This highly Erasmian passage on the importance of things (*res*) as opposed to words (*verba*) is an echo of Montaigne's essay "De l'institution des enfans [Of the Institution and Education of Children]" (Villey, ed., 1.26 [trans. Florio, 25], esp. 168–173 [trans. Florio, 1: 178–184]).

[29] Aeschines and Calvus: two celebrated orators of antiquity—the first, the rival of Demosthenes, the second, of Cicero.

N'ont-ils pas aussi raison, je vous prie, qui, pour huict ou dix motz qui leur sembleront estrangers ou hardis ou quelque maniere de parler Gasconne, en cet ouvrage celeste par tout et au langage mesme, suiveront l'exemple de celuy qui, contemplant à loisir Venus toute nüe, ne feit semblant ny d'admirer ny de dire mot, jusques à ce qu'un fil bigarré, peut estre, qu'il apperceut au tissu de son ceston, luy feit envie de parler pour mesdire? Quand je le deffends de telles charges, je me mocque: prions-les que, pour luy reprocher plus plaisamment ses erreurs, ils se mettent à les contrefaire. Qu'ilz nous forgent cent vocables à leur poste, pourveu qu'un en die trois ou quatre ordinaires: et vocables[23] qui percent où les autres frayent simplement. Qu'ilz nous representent mille nouvelles phrases qui dient en demy ligne le subject, le succez et la louange de quelque chose; tres belles, delicates, vifves, et vivifiantes phrases; mille metaphores esgalement admirables et inouyes; mille trespropres applications de motz enforcis et approfondis, à divers et nouveaux sens (car voilà l'innovation que j'y treuve et qui, si c'est par la grace de Dieu celle qu'on craint, n'est pas au moins celle qu'on imite); et tout cela, dis-je, sans qu'un Lecteur y puisse rien accuser que nouveauté, mais bien Françoise. Lors nous leur permettrons de nous attribuer leurs escritz, affin de les descharger de la honte qu'ils encourroient d'en porter le tiltre.

Or, à mesure que jardiner à propos une langue est un plus bel œuvre, à mesure est-il permettable à moins de gens, comme dict mon Pere[24]. C'est à quelques jeunes courtisans, sans parler de tant d'escrivains, qu'il faudroit donner de l'argent pour ne s'en mesler plus, lesquels ne cherchent pas d'innover pour amender, mais d'empirer pour innover: et, qui pis est, avec condemnation des vieux vocables, qui sont ou meilleurs ou, s'ils sont egaux, doivent encores estre preferez par l'usage[25], et, apres tout, qui ne se peuvent rejetter qu'au mespris de l'apprentissage de nostre langue entre les estrangers, pour ne la pouvoir

---

[23] Le texte original donne «vocales» pour «vocables».
[24] «Laissons le à ceux qui en font profession expresse» (I, 26, 168 A).
[25] Cette condamnation des néologismes au nom de l'usage est un poncif de la Renaissance. Cf. Rabelais, *Pantagruel*, chapitre VI, et Montaigne: «Au langage, la recherche des frases nouvelles et de mots peu cogneuz vient d'une ambition puerile et pedantesque» (I, 26, 172 C).

Are not they also in the right, I ask you, who for eight or ten words that seem to them foreign or daring or some kind of Gascon expression in that work, which is sublime throughout, and even in its language, will follow the example of him who, contemplating at his leisure the naked Venus, makes a show of not admiring and of not saying a word, until perhaps a clashing thread, which he spots in the material of her girdle, moves him to speak in order to disparage? When I defend him against such charges, I am full of scorn: let us hope that, so as to reproach him for his errors more comically, they take to imitating them. Let them forge for us a hundred new words to their liking, provided that someone speaks three or four ordinary ones—and words[30] that pierce where the others merely grate. Let them display for us a thousand new turns of phrase that would express the question in half a line—the realization and the praise of something; most lovely, delicate, lively, and enlivening phrases; a thousand metaphors equally admirable and unheard-of; a thousand highly accurate applications of words pushed to the limit and well studied in various and new senses (for that is the innovation that I find there, which, if it is the sort, as God will have it, that one fears, is no less the sort that is imitated). And all this, I say, without a reader's being able to condemn in it anything except novelty—but novelty, indeed, in French. Then we shall allow them to bestow their writings on us, so that they may be cleared of the shame they have incurred by being responsible for such work.

Now, to the extent that cultivating a language properly is a lovely activity, it is allowable to fewer persons, as my Father says.[31] Certain young courtiers (not to mention so many writers) should be paid not to meddle with it: those who seek, not to innovate in order to improve, but to degrade in order to innovate—and, what is worse, while condemning old expressions that either are better or, if of equal quality, ought still to be preferred on account of usage.[32] And these, after all, cannot be rejected without making foreigners scorn to learn our

---

[30] For "vocables" [words], the original text reads "vocales."

[31] "Laissons le à ceux qui en font profession expresse [Let us leave it to those, whose profession is to doe nothing else]" (Villey, ed., 1.26.168[A]; trans. Florio, 1: 179).

[32] This condemnation of neologisms in the name of usage is a commonplace in the Renaissance. Cf. Rabelais, *Pantagruel*, chap. 6, and Montaigne: "au langage, la recherche des frases nouvelles et de mots peu cogneuz vient d'une ambition puerile et pedantesque [in common speech, for one to hunt after new phrases, and unaccustomed-quaint words, proceedeth of a scholasticall and childish ambition]" (Villey, ed., 1.26.172[C]; trans. Florio, 1: 183).

happer non plus que Prothée[26] et, d'abondant, à la ruine des livres qui les ont employez. Ilz ont beau faire, pourtant, on se mocquera bien de nostre sottise à nous autres, quand nous dirons: son «lever», son «col», sa «servitude», au lieu de leurs nouveaux termes: son «habiller», son «coulx», son «esclavitude», et semblables importantes corrections; mais quand ilz viendront à chocquer avec le temps Amiot et Ronsard sur ces mots là, qu'ilz s'attendent de perdre les arsons[27]. Pour descrire le langage des *Essais*, il le faut transcrire; il n'ennuye jamais le Lecteur, que quand il cesse: et tout y est parfaict, sauf la fin. Les Dieux et les Deesses donnerent leur langue à ce livre ou desormais ils ont pris la sienne. C'est le clou qui fixera la volubilité de nostre idiome, continue jusques icy: son credit qui s'eslevera jour à jour jusques au ciel, empeschant que de temps en temps on ne trouve suranné ce que nous disons

---

[26] Protée: monstre marin à forme changeante, devenu l'emblème de la mutation. Cf. Erasme, «Proteo mutabilior», *Adages*, II, 2, 74.

[27] Jacques Amyot (1513-1593), traducteur des *Vies des hommes illustres* et des *Œuvres morales* de Plutarque. Montaigne lui donne «la palme» parmi tous les écrivains français «pour la naïfveté [le naturel] et pureté du langage» (II, 4, 363 A). Montaigne sait gré aussi à Ronsard d'avoir «donné credit à nostre poësie Françoise» (I, 26, 171 A) dans une langue proche de la «perfection ancienne» (II, 17, 661 A).

language, because they would be able to get no better hold of it than of Proteus,[33] and, what is more, at the cost of ruining those books that have employed them. But whatever such people may do, the stupidity of the rest of us will be mocked, when we say, his "lever" [rising], his "col" [neck],[34] his "servitude," instead of their new terms: his "habiller" [dressing], his "coulx," his "esclavitude," and similar weighty corrections. But when they shall come, in time, to run up against Amyot and Ronsard with those words, let them look to be tossed from their saddles.[35] The language of the *Essays*, to be described, must be transcribed; it never wearies the reader, except when it ceases, and everything about it is perfect but its coming to an end. The gods and goddesses gave their language to this book, from which, henceforth, they took its own. This work is the nail that will fix the mutability of our speech, which continues to this moment: it is this work's authority that will mount day by day to the heavens, preventing us from sometimes finding things that we say today outworn, since it will persist in saying

---

[33] Proteus: a water monster of changeable form, who became the emblem of mutability. Cf. Erasmus, "Proteo mutabilior" (*Adages*, 2.2.74 [*Collected Works of Erasmus*, vol. 33, trans. and annotated R. A. B. Mynors {Toronto: University of Toronto Press, 1991}, 113–114]).

[34] Ironically, this is one of the words Marie de Gournay eliminated, seemingly on account of its archaism, when she partially rewrote Ronsard's "La harangue du Duc de Guise aux soldats de Metz" in 1624 (see Ilsley, *Daughter of the Renaissance*, 138).

[35] Jacques Amyot (1513–1593), translator of the *Lives* and *Moralia* of Plutarch. Montaigne gives him "la palme [pricke and praise]" amongst all French writers "pour la naïfveté et pureté du langage [for his natural purity, and pure elegancie of the tongue]" (Villey, ed., 2.4.363[A]; trans. Florio, 2: 42). Montaigne is also grateful to Ronsard for having "donné credit à nostre poésie Françoise [raised our French Poesie unto that height of honour, where it now is]" (Villey, ed., 1.26.171[A]; trans. Florio, 1: 181) in a language close to the "perfection ancienne [ancient perfection]" (Villey, ed., 2.17.661[A]; trans. Florio, 2: 389).

aujourd'huy, parce qu'il perseverera de le dire, et le faisant juger bon d'autant qu'il sera sien.

On le reprend apres de la licence de ses parolles, contre la ceremonie, dont il s'est si bien revengé luy mesme qu'il a deschargé chacun d'en prendre la peine[28]. Aussi n'oserions nous dire si nous pensons ou non qu'un homme soit plus habille pour establir la pratique de l'amour legitime, honneste, et sacramentalle, et sa theorique horrible et diffamable; et nous leur accordons en fin qu'il soit meschant, execrable, et damnable, d'oser prester la langue ou l'oreille à l'expression de ce subject; mais qu'il soit impudique, on leur nye. Car outre que ce livre prouve fort bien le macquerellage que les loix de la ceremonie prestent à Venus, quelz autheurs de pudicité sont ceux-cy, je vous prie, qui vont encherissant si hault la force et la grace des effectz de Cupidon, que de faire accroire à la jeunesse qu'on n'en peut pas ouyr seulement parler sans transport? S'ilz le content à des femmes, n'ont elles pas raison de mettre leur abstinence en garde contre un Prescheur qui soustient qu'on ne peut seulement ouyr parler de la table sans rompre son jeusne? Quoy donc: Socrates, qui se levoit continent d'aupres cette belle et brillante flamme

---

[28] Montaigne critique la «ceremonie» (les obligations sociales) au début de l'essai «De la Præsumption»: «Nous ne sommes que ceremonie. [...] La ceremonie nous defend d'exprimer par paroles les choses licites et naturelles» (II, 17, 632 A).

them, causing them to be judged good inasmuch as they shall be its own.³⁶

He is reproached, next, for the license of his speech, contrary to social niceties—for which he has revenged himself so thoroughly that he has relieved everyone of the trouble of doing so.³⁷ Moreover, we would not dare to say whether or not we think that a man is more capable for establishing a legitimate, honorable, and sacramental practice of love, when his theory is horrible and defamatory; and we grant them, in the end, that it is wicked, execrable, and damnable to dare to lend tongue or ear to the expression of this subject; but that he is obscene, we deny them. For besides the fact that this book demonstrates amply the bawd's services that the rules of social politeness perform on behalf of Venus, what advocates of chastity are these authors, I ask you, who go about so bidding up the strength and the grace of the effects of Cupid that they lead young people to believe that one cannot even hear them spoken of without being transported? If they tell this to women, aren't women right to put their abstinence on guard against a preacher who maintains that one cannot merely hear the table spoken of without breaking one's fast? What, then? Did Socrates, who rose continent from

---

³⁶ In the original, "son" in "son credit," "il" in "parce qu'il perseverera de le dire," and "sien" in "d'autant qu'il sera sien" may refer equally to the "livre" or to its author. It is especially paradoxical that on this point Marie de Gournay resoundingly ("nail" = "clou") turns Montaigne's own words against him:

> J'escris mon livre à peu d'hommes et à peu d'années. Si ç'eust esté une matiere de durée, il l'eust fallu commettre à un langage plus ferme. Selon la variation continuelle qui a suyvi le nostre jusques à cette heure, qui peut esperer que sa forme presente soit en usage, d'icy à cinquante ans? . . . Je n'ay garde de l'en tenir là tant qu'il fuira et se difformera comme il faict. C'est aux bons et utiles escrits de le clouer à eux. . . .

> [I write my booke to few men, and to few yeares. Had it beene a matter of lasting continuance, it should have beene compiled in a better and more polished language: According to the continuall variation, that hitherto hath followed our French tongue, who may hope, that it's present forme shall be in use fifty yeares hence? . . . It lies not in my power, so long as it glideth and differeth and altereth as it doth, to keepe it at a stay. It is for excellent and profitable compositions to fasten it unto them. . . .]   (Villey, ed., 3.9.982[B,C]; trans. Florio, 3: 229)

³⁷ Montaigne critiques "ceremonie" (social obligations) at the opening of the essay "De la præsumption [Of Presumption]": "Nous ne sommes que ceremonie. . . . La ceremonie nous defend d'exprimer par parolles les choses licites et naturelles [We are nought but ceremonie. . . . Ceremonie forbids us by words to express lawfull and naturall things]" (Villey, ed., 2.17.632[A]; trans. Florio, 2: 355–356).

d'amour dont la Græce, à ce qu'on disoit, n'eust sçeu porter deux, faisoit-il alors moins preuve de chasteté par ce qu'il avoit ouy, veu, dict et touché que ne faisoit Timon se promenant seul tandis en un desert[29]?

Livia selon l'opinion des sages, parloit en grande et suffisante Dame, comme elle estoit, disant qu'à une femme chaste un homme nud n'est

---

[29] Timon d'Athènes, le type même du misanthrope. Cf. I, 50, 304 A.

beside that beautiful and brilliant flame of love, of whom Greece,[38] it was said, could not have borne two, show at that time less proof of chastity because he had heard, seen, spoken, and touched than Timon did, who was then strolling alone in a desert?[39]

Livia, in the opinion of the wise, spoke like a great and sufficient Lady, such as she was, in saying that to a chaste woman a naked man is

---

[38] In her edition of the Preface of 1599, Franchetti remarks (183 n. 18) that the reading "Grece" corrects "grace" in the 1595 version. In fact, the earlier version reads "Græce," and Professor Rigolot has corrected his edition accordingly for this volume.

[39] Timon of Athens, the very type of misanthropy—to the point that it came naturally to Marguerite de Valois to urge her husband, the King of Navarre (and future Henri IV of France) to join her at the Parisian court in the following terms: "si vous estiez honneste homme, vous quitteriez l'agriculture et l'humeur de Timon pour venir vivre parmi les hommes" [if you were a man of virtue and refinement, you would give up rural pursuits and the humor of Timon and come live amongst men] (*Mémoires et autres écrits de Marguerite de Valois, La Reine Margot*, ed. Yves Cazaux [Paris: Mercure de France, 1986], 236). Cf. Villey, ed., 1.50.304(A); trans. Florio, 1: 344.

The reference to Socrates must allude to Alcibiades' account in Plato's *Symposium* of having attempted to seduce the philosopher by means of his physical beauty:

> ... I put my thick cloak over him (it was winter) and lay down under his short cloak. I put my arms around this remarkable, wonderful man—he is, you know— and lay there with him all night long.... And after all that, he spurned and disdained and scorned my charms so thoroughly, and treated me so brutally ... that I got up the next morning, after having spent the night with Socrates, and for all the naughtiness we'd got up to, I might as well have been sleeping with my father or an elder brother.   (trans. Robin Waterfield, World's Classics [Oxford: Oxford University Press, 1994], 66 [218b-d])

The beauty of Alcibiades was legendary—see, e.g., *Plutarch's Lives*, ed. and trans. Bernadotte Perrin, Loeb Classical Library (Cambridge, MA: Harvard University Press; London: Heinemann, 1916), 4: 4–5 (*Alcibiades* 1.3-4), of which Montaigne had made use in the translation of Amyot (see Villey, ed., *passim*). This particular story, moreover, was widely known, being mentioned also by Petronius in *Satyricon* (trans. Michael Heseltine, Loeb Classical Library [London: Heinemann; New York: Macmillan, 1913], 286–287 [128]) and Cornelius Nepos in his life of Alcibiades (*The Great Generals of Foreign Nations*, 7). The latter work, which had appeared in a Paris edition in 1569 and was also drawn on by Montaigne (see Villey, ed., *passim*), contains a passage that may have influenced Marie de Gournay:

> In this man Nature seems to have tried to see what she could accomplish; for it is agreed by all who have written his biography that he was never excelled either in faults or in virtues.
>   (*Cornelius Nepos*, trans. John C. Rolfe, Loeb Classical Library
>   [London: Heineman; New York: Putnam's, 1929], 435 [1])

Socrates is mentioned shortly afterwards (436–437 [2]). Alcibiades also figures in the story of Timon. Cf. below, 53 and n. 43.

non plus qu'un image[30]. Elle jugeoit, ou qu'il faut que le monde bannisse du tout l'Amour et sa mere hors de ses limites, ou que, s'il les y retient, c'est pipperie et batellerie, de faire la chaste pour les sequestrer de la langue, des yeux et des oreilles, voire batellerie à ceux mesmes qui n'en ont point d'usage; d'autant qu'outre cela que l'ouyr et veoir et dire n'est rien, ilz advouent qu'ilz y ont au moins part, ou presomptifve ou louablement acceptable, par le mariage. N'eust elle pas aussi volontiers dict que les femmes, qui crient qu'on les violle par les oreilles ou par les yeux, le feissent à dessein, affin de pretendre cause d'ignorance de se mal garder par ailleurs? La plus legitime consideration qu'elles y puissent apporter, c'est de craindre qu'on ne les tente par là; mais elles doivent avoir grand'honte de confesser ne se sentir de bon or que jusques à la couppelle, et pudiques que pour ce qu'elles ne trouvent qui voulust employer l'impudicité. L'assault est le hazard du combattant; mais il est aussi le triumphe du vainqueur. Toute vertu desire l'espreuve, comme tenant son essence mesme du contraste. Le plus fascheux malheur qui puisse arriver à Polydamas et Theagenes[31], c'est de ne rencontrer personne pour envier, qui la puissante palaestre de l'un, qui la viste course de l'autre, affin de se dresser un trophée de leur cheute. Non seulement par ambition de faire sentir sa vertu une femme sage ne fuit pas la recherche, mais encore plus par juste recognoissance de la foible condition humaine, elle l'appete: pour ne s'oser asseurer de sa continence qu'elle n'en ait une fois refusé la richesse, une autre fois la beauté, les graces et

---

[30] «Aussi disoit Livia [Livie, femme d'Auguste] qu'à une femme de bien un homme nud n'est non plus qu'une image [une statue]» (III, 5, 860 B).
[31] Allusion aux promesses de Polydamas, célèbre athlète d'une force prodigieuse (Pausanias, *Description de la Grèce*, VI, 5) et à celles de Théagène, héros du roman grec d'Héliodore, *Théagène et Chariclée*, ou les *Ethiopiques* (IIIe s. apr. J.-C.), traduit en français par Amyot.

just a statue.⁴⁰ It was her opinion that either the world must banish Love and his mother entirely beyond its borders, or that, if it retains them, it is trickery and foolishness to play the chaste woman by keeping them from the tongue, the eyes, and the ears—indeed, foolishness even for those who do not indulge themselves, inasmuch as, besides the fact that hearing, seeing, and speaking are nothing, they admit that they at least partake in such pleasures, either presumptively or in a praiseworthy and acceptable fashion, through marriage. Did she not also freely say that women who cry out that they are being raped by the ears or the eyes do so on purpose, so as to give themselves the excuse of ignorance for protecting themselves poorly elsewhere? The most legitimate reason they can adduce is the fear of being tempted in this way; but they must be thoroughly ashamed to confess that they feel themselves to be true gold only up to the point of the assay, and that they are decent only because they have not found anyone who wished to be indecent with them. The assault puts the combatant in peril, but it is also the triumph of the victor. Every virtue longs to be put to the test, as if deriving its very essence from contrast. The most provoking annoyance possible for Polydamas and Theagenes⁴¹ would be to encounter no one who would envy the powerful wrestling of the one, the swift race of the other, so as to set up their downfall as a trophy for himself. Not only does a wise woman, out of ambition to sense her own virtue, not shrink from the pursuit, but—all the more because of a true recognition of the feeble human condition—she desires it; for she does not dare to assure herself of her continence unless she has on one occasion refused wealth, on another beauty, charm, and her own desires. Let the

---

⁴⁰ Livia was the wife of Augustus. Cf. *Essais*: "Aussi disoit Livia qu'à une femme de bien un homme nud n'est non plus qu'une image [And *Livia* said, that to an honest woman, a naked man is no more then an Image]" (Villey, ed., 3.5.860[B]; trans. Florio, 3: 85); also, from "De la præsumption [Of Presumption]," "Nous avons apris aux Dames de rougir oyant seulement nommer ce qu'elles ne craignent aucunement à faire; nous n'osons appeller à droict nos membres, et ne craignons pas de les employer à toute sorte de desbauche. [Wee have taught Ladies to blush, onely by hearing that named, which they nothing feare to doe. Wee dare not call our members by their proper names, and feare not to employ them in all kind of dissoluteness.]" (Villey, ed., 2.17.632[A]; trans. Florio, 2: 355–356).

⁴¹ Allusion to the undertakings of Polydamas, a famous athlete of prodigious strength (Pausanias, *Description of Greece*, trans. W. H. S. Jones, Loeb Classical Library [Cambridge, MA: Harvard University Press; London: Heinemann, 1933], 3: 32–33 [6.5.7]) and to those of Theagenes, the hero of the Greek novel by Heliodorus, *Theagenes and Chariclea, or the Aethiopica* (third century A.D.), which was first published in 1534 (the manuscript having been discovered only eight years before) and had been translated into French by Amyot. It is in Book Four that Theagenes, inspired by love, responds to the general challenge of Ormenos to a foot race, in which he triumphs.

ses propres desirs. Laissez parler le poursuivant à telle oreille, et plaindre et prier et crier, cette mesme gravité qui l'arme contre les faulces persuasions, ce sot et ridicule vice de la legere creance et les erreurs contre la saincte religion de ses peres, l'arme encore contre cette batterie.

Quant à l'obscurité, qu'on reprend apres en noz *Essais,* je n'en diray que ce mot: c'est que, puisque la matiere n'est pas aussi bien pour les novices, il leur a deu suffire d'accommoder le stile à la portée des profez seulement. On ne peut traicter les grandes choses selon l'intelligence des petits; car la comprehension des hommes ne va guere outre leur invention. Ce n'est pas icy le rudiment des apprentifs; c'est l'Alcoran des maistres, la quinte essence de la philosophie: œuvre non à gouster mais à digerer et chylifier, le dernier livre qu'on doit prendre et le dernier qu'on doit quicter. Ilz galoppent apres ses discours couppez, extravagans, et sans obligation de traicter un poinct tout entier, et je sens bien qu'on me va mettre de son escot en cette fricassée de resveries diverses[32]. Surquoy je les prie de faire une liste à leur gré d'autant d'autres subjetz qu'il en comprend, pour dire sur chacun non peu, suivant l'exemple des *Essais,* mais un seul mot, pourveu que ce soit tousjours le mieux qui s'y puisse dire, ainsi que mon Pere a faict; et lors je leur prometz que non seulement je leur pardonneray, mais que j'ay recouvré maistre en eux, comme cet ancien en Socrates[33].

---

[32] «Cette fricassée de resveries diverses»: l'expression est très montaignienne. Cf. III, 13, 1079 B; et I, 26, 146 A; II, 10, 409 A; II, 18, 665 C; III, 11, 1033 B.

[33] «Cet ancien en Socrates»: probablement Alcibiade dans le *Banquet* de Platon. Montaigne cite le récit d'Alcibiade au sujet de Socrate au début des «Coches» (III, 6, 899–900 B).

pursuer speak in such an ear and complain and pray and cry—that same gravity that arms her against false persuasions, the foolish and ridiculous vice of easy credence, and errors against the holy religion of her fathers arms her also against this battering.

As for the obscurity that is next taken to task in our *Essays*, I shall say nothing about it but this: that since the matter is so poorly suited to novices, they had no choice but to accommodate their style to the capacity of experts. One cannot deal with great affairs according to small intelligences; for the understanding of men hardly goes beyond their invention. Here is not the elementary knowledge of an apprentice but the Koran of the masters, the quintessence of philosophy: a work not to taste but to digest and absorb, the last work one should take up and the last to put down. They gallop after his arguments, which are truncated, digressive, and without obligation to deal with a point as a whole; and I have the feeling that I will be tarred with the same brush when it comes to this stew of diverse fantasies.[42] In this regard, I beg them to make a list at will of as many different subjects as he includes, then to make about each of them, not a few statements, on the example of the *Essays*, but a single one, provided that it should always be the best that may be pronounced, just as my Father has done; and then, I assure them, not only will I forgive them, but I will have recovered a master in them, as that ancient man did in Socrates.[43]

---

[42] "Cette fricassée de resveries diverses." The expression is highly characteristic of Montaigne. Cf. Villey, ed., 3.13.1079(B) (trans. Florio, 3: 339); 1.26.146(A) (trans. Florio, 1: 148); 2.10.409(A) (trans. Florio, 2: 94); 2.18.665(C) (trans. Florio, 2: 392); 3.11.1033(B) (trans. Florio, 3: 286).

[43] "That ancient man ... in Socrates": possibly Alcibiades in the *Symposium*. Montaigne cites Alcibiades' account of Socrates at the opening of the essay "Des coches [Of Coaches]" (Villey, ed., 3.6.899–900[B]; trans. Florio, 3: 129–130). That account, however, portrays Socrates' calm resolution in the face of physical danger. Marie de Gournay's wording ("j'ay recouvré maistre en eux, comme cet ancien en Socrates") and focus on wisdom might rather recall "De l'experience [Of Experience]":

C'est par mon experience que j'accuse l'humaine ignorance, qui est, à mon advis, le plus seur party de l'escole du monde. Ceux qui ne la veulent conclurre en eux par un si vain exemple que le mien ou que le leur, qu'ils la recognoissent par Socrates, le maistre des maistres. Car le philosophe Antisthenes à ses disciples: Allons, disoit-il, vous et moy ouyr Socrates; là je seray disciple avec vous.

[It is by my experience I accuse humane ignorance, which (in mine opinion) is the surest part of the Worlds schoole. Those that will not conclude it in themselves, by so vaine an example as mine, or theirs, let them acknowledge it by *Socrates*, the Maister of Maisters. For the Philosopher *Antisthenes*, was wont to say to his Disciples: Come on my Maisters, let you and me goe to heare *Socrates*. There shall I be a fellow Disciple with you.]

(Villey, ed., 3.13.1075–1076 [B,C]; trans. Florio, 3: 335)

54　PRÉFACE DE 1595

Ceux qui pretendent calomnier sa religion, pour avoir si meritoirement inscript un heretique au rolle des excellens poetes de ce temps[34], ou sur quelque autre punctille de pareil air, monstrent assez qu'ilz cherchent à trouver des compagnons en la desbauche de la leur. C'est à moy d'en parler, car moy seulle avois la parfaicte cognoissance de cette grande ame, et c'est à moy d'en estre creue de bonne foy, quand ce livre ne l'esclairciroit pas, comme ayant quitté tant de magnifiques, pompeuses et plausibles vertus, dont le monde se brave affin d'enchoir au reproche de niaiserie que me font mes compagnes, pour n'avoir rien en partage que l'innocence et la sincerité. Je dis doncq avec verité certaine que tout ainsi que jamais homme ne voulut plus de mal aux nulles et faulces religions que luy, de mesme il n'en fut oncques un plus ennemy de tout ce qui blessoit le respect de la vraye; et la touche de celle-cy c'estoit, et pour luy comme les *Essais* declarent, et pour moy sa creature, la saincte loy des peres[35]. Qui pourroit aussi supporter ces Titans escheleurs de

---

[34] Théodore de Bèze (1519–1605) disciple et successeur de Calvin. A Rome on avait reproché à Montaigne «d'avoir nommé des poëtes heretiques» dans ses *Essais* (*Journal de voyage*, éd. cit., p. 222). Il avait fait l'éloge de Théodore de Bèze et de George Buchanan (I, 25 et II, 17) et devait protester contre un reproche qu'il estimait injuste (III, 10).

[35] Dans l'essai «Des Prieres» Montaigne déclare vouloir s'en tenir aux «sainctes prescriptions de l'Eglise catholique, apostolique et Romaine» (I, 56, 318 C).

Those who maintain that, for having so deservedly enrolled a heretic in the register of the excellent poets of his time,[44] or for some other such trivial matter, he has slandered his religion show clearly enough that they seek companions in debauching their own. It is I who have the right to speak in this regard, for I alone was perfectly acquainted with that great soul, and it is I who have the right to be trusted on this subject when that book does not clarify it, as someone who has relinquished so many magnificent, rich, and admired virtues, which the world glories in, to incur the reproach of silliness from my fellow women for having nothing to my lot but innocence and sincerity. I say with certain truth, therefore, that just as no man ever bore such ill will towards worthless and false religions as he, so none was ever a greater enemy to all that impaired respect for the true one; and the touchstone of that religion was, both for him, as the *Essays* declare, and for me, his creature, the holy law of the fathers.[45] Who, moreover, could tolerate those heaven-climbing Titans that think to arrive at God by their own

---

[44] Théodore de Bèze (1519–1605), disciple and successor of Calvin. In Rome, Montaigne was reproached "d'avoir nommé des poëtes heretiques" [for having named heretical poets] in his *Essais* (*Journal de voyage*, ed. Garavini, 222). He had praised Théodore de Bèze and George Buchanan (see Villey, ed., 1.26.174[A] [trans. Florio, 1: 185–186] and 2.17.661[A] [trans. Florio, 2: 388]) and was compelled to protest against a reproach that he considered unjust: "Et ne conceday pas au magistrat mesme qu'il eust raison de condamner un livre pour avoir logé entre les meilleurs poëtes de ce siecle un heretique [I would not give the magistrate my voice, that he had reason to condemne a booke, because an heretick was therein named and extolled to be one of the best Poets of this age]" (Villey, ed., 3.10.1013[C]; trans. Florio, 3: 264).

[45] In the essay "Des prieres [Of Prayers and Orisons]," Montaigne declares that he wishes to confine himself to the "sainctes prescriptions de l'Eglise catholique, apostolique et Romaine [holy prescriptions of the Catholike, Apostolike, and Romane Church]" (Villey, ed., 1.56.318[C]; trans. Florio, 1: 358).

Ciel, qui pensent arriver à Dieu par leurs moyens, et circonscrire ses œuvres aux limites de leur raison[36]? Nous disons, au lieu, que là mesme où toutes choses sont plus incroyables, là sont plus certainement les faictz de Dieu, et que Dieu n'est çà, ne là, s'il n'y a miracle. Icy principalement le faut-il escouter d'aguet, et se garder de broncher sur cette libre et brusque façon de s'exprimer, nonchallante et parfois, ce semble, designante d'attiser un calomniateur affin que, puisqu'estant des-ja meschant, il nous est justement odieux, il se declare encore un sot pour son interpretation cornuë, dont nous ayons le plaisir de le voir diffamé de deux vices.

M'amuseray-je à particulariser quelques regles pour se gouverner en cette lecture? suffit de dire en un mot: «Ne t'en mesle pas», ou «sois sage». Je rendz graces à Dieu que parmy la confusion de tant de creances effrenées, qui traversent et tempestent son Eglise, il luy ait pleu de l'estaier d'un si ferme et si puissant pillier. Ayant besoin de fortifier la foy des simples contre telz assaultz, il a pensé ne le pouvoir mieux faire qu'en produisant une ame qui n'eust eu semblable depuis quatorze ou quinze cens ans, pour la verifier de son approbation. Si la religion Catholique, à la naissance de cet enfant, eust sçeu combien grand il devoit estre un jour, quelle apprehension eust esté la sienne de l'avoir pour adversaire, quelz vœux n'eust elle offertz affin de l'avoir pour suffragant? Il s'agissoit à bon escient de ses affaires, alors que Dieu deliberoit s'il

---

[36] Les Titans, fils de la Terre, firent trembler le palais de Saturne. Cf. Horace, *Odes* II, XII, 6, et Montaigne, II, 12, 533 B. Ici les Titans désignent les «esprits forts», pris à partie dans l'*Apologie de Raymond Sebon* (II, 12).

means and circumscribe His works by the limits of their reason?[46] Instead, we say that precisely where things are more incredible they are more certainly the workings of God, and that God is neither here nor there if there is no miracle. Here chiefly one must prick up one's ears to hear him and keep from flinching at that free and brusque way of expressing himself, casual and sometimes, it seems, intent on inflaming a slanderer in order that, since the latter is already justly odious to us for his ill-will, he may further expose himself as a fool for his outlandish interpretation, with the result that we have the pleasure of seeing him discredited for two vices.

Shall I busy myself in spelling out some rules to follow in this reading? It's enough simply to say, "Don't meddle!" or "Listen to reason!" I give thanks to God that amidst the confusion of so many unbridled opinions that blow through and bluster at His church, it has pleased Him to sustain it with so firm and powerful a pillar. Needing to fortify the faith of the simple against such assaults, He thought that he could not do so more effectively than by producing a soul who (in order to confirm His approbation of it), would not have had its equal for fourteen or fifteen hundred years. If the Catholic religion, at the birth of that child, had known how great he was bound to be one day, what apprehension would it have felt about having him as its adversary, what vows would it not have offered to have him as its champion? Its affairs were indeed at issue when God considered whether He would give such

---

[46] The Titans, sons of the earth, made the palace of Saturn tremble. Cf. Horace, *Odes* 2.12.6-9, cited by Montaigne in the "Apologie de Raimond Sebond [An Apologie of *Raymond Sebond*]" (Villey, ed., 2.12.533[B]; trans. Florio, 2: 240), in which, like Marie de Gournay here, he attacks those who dare to pronounce boldly regarding religious mysteries. Horace's account of the Titans in *Odes* 3.4.42-48 would particularly have encouraged such an application:

> ... scimus, ut impios
> Titanas immanemque turbam
>   fulmine sustulerit caduco,
>
> qui terram inertam, qui mare temperat
> ventosum et urbes regnaque tristia,
>   divosque mortalesque turmas
>   imperio regit unus aequo.

[Full well we know how the impious Titans and their frightful horde were struck down with the descending bolt by him who rules the lifeless earth, the wind-swept sea, cities, and the gloomy realms below, who alone with righteous sway governs the gods and throngs of men.]

(*Horace, Odes and Epodes*, trans. C. E. Bennett, rev. ed., Loeb Classical Library [Cambridge, MA: Harvard University Press; London: Heinemann, 1927], 188-191)

donneroit un si digne present à un siecle si indigne, ou si sa bonté l'appelleroit à l'amendement par un si noble exemple. Personne n'eust pensé qu'il y eust eu faute aux nouvelles religions si le grand Montaigne les eust admises, ou nul de ceux mesmes à qui la faute eust esté congnuë n'eust eu honte de la commettre apres luy. Certes, il a rendu vraye sa proposition, que des tres-grandes et des tres-simples ames se faisoyent les bien croyans, comme aussi la mienne, que de ces deux extremitez se faisoyent les gens de bien. Je tiens le party de ceux qui jugent que le vice procede de sottise et, consequemment, que plus on approche de la suffisance, plus on s'eslongne de luy.

Quelle teste bien faicte[37] ne fieroit à Platon sa bourse et son secret, ayant seulement leu ses livres? En cette consideration je mesprisay le reproche d'imprudence et bigerrerie, dont on me chargeoit lors que je le cherissois sur ses *Essais,* avant que l'avoir veu ny pratiqué. Toute amitié, disois-je, est mal fondée s'elle ne l'est sur la suffisance et vertu du subject. Or si la suffisance paroist non seulement en ce livre, mais s'elle y paroist en telle mesure, et le vice n'y peut escheoir; et, par consequent, il ne serviroit à rien de differer d'aymer jusques à l'entreveuë, qui ne chercheroit l'amour au lieu de l'amitié, ou qui n'auroit honte qu'on dist que sa raison eust plus de force que ses sens à nouer une alliance, et qu'il peut bien faire s'il avoit les yeux fermés? Nous avons des tesmoignages de vertu de tous ces anciens philosophes egaulx à ceux de leur entendement, par lequel ilz se survivent eux mesmes et constituent apres tant de siecles des loix à l'univers: soit des tesmoignages en leurs propres livres, soit, pour ceux à qui le temps les a raviz, en la relation des escritz de leurs compagnons. J'excepte Cæsar seulement en toute la sequelle des Muses, pour ame egalement forte et perdue. Je sçay bien qu'on me

---

[37] Montaigne demandait de «choisir un conducteur [précepteur] qui eust plutost *la teste bien faicte* que bien pleine» (I, 26, 150 A).

a worthy gift to such an unworthy age or whether, out of His goodness, He would urge it to amendment by such a noble example. No one would have thought that there was anything wrong with the new religions if the great Montaigne had allowed them; nor would any, even amongst those whose fault would have become known, have been ashamed to commit it following his example. Certainly, he has proved the truth of his proposition that true believers are made from the greatest and the simplest souls, as also of mine that good people are made out of these two extremities. I hold with those who judge that vice proceeds from foolishness and, consequently, that the closer one comes to sufficiency, the more one draws away from it.

What well-tempered mind[47] would not entrust his purse and his secret to Plato, having merely read his books? Out of this consideration, I disdained the accusation of imprudence and caprice levelled against me when I valued him on the basis of his *Essays* before having seen or visited him. Every friendship, I said, is founded poorly if not on the sufficiency and virtue of the person in question. Now if sufficiency does not merely appear in that book but appears in such measure, not only can vice not come into it but, consequently, it would serve no purpose to put off liking him until an interview for someone who would not be seeking love in the place of friendship, or who would not be ashamed to have it said that his reason exerted more strength than his senses in forming a bond and that he could do well if he had his eyes closed. We have testimonies of virtue from all those ancient philosophers equal to the testimonies of their intelligence, by means of which they have outlived themselves and, after so many centuries, constitute universal laws: whether testimonials in their own books or, for those whose books have been snatched away by time, in written accounts by their companions. I except only Caesar in the whole train of the Muses, as a soul equally

---

[47] Montaigne recommended "choisir un conducteur qui eust plutost la teste bien faicte que bien pleine [chusing (a) director, whom I would rather commend for having a well composed and temperate braine, than a full stuft head]" (Villey, ed., 1.26.150[A]; trans. Florio, 1: 154–155).

demandera s'il y a point eu de grandz hommes entre eux qui n'ont embrassé les lettres. Respondons: La nature, impatiente d'inutilité, rejette l'oisiveté de ses parties et ne les peut arrester encore sur un office qui n'arrive pas au plus loing de leur portée. Deffendez pour veoir à la vigueur de Milon[38] l'extreme exercice des forces corporelles, ou celuy de l'allegresse à la legereté d'Achilles[39]. Cela estant, il faut veoir si, hors les lettres qu'ilz disoient la philosophie, il y auroit point quelque

---

[38] Milon de Crotone, célèbre athlète grec (dernière partie du VIᵉ siècle av. J.-C.).
[39] L'affection entre Achille et Patrocle est évoquée dans l'essai «De l'Amitié» (I, 28, 187 C).

strong and lost.[48] I am fully aware that I will be asked if there have not been great men amongst them who did not take up letters. Let us reply: Nature, impatient of uselessness, rejects the idleness of its members and cannot keep them in a function that does not attain to the utmost of their reach. To try this out, forbid to the vigor of Milon[49] the extreme exercise of bodily strength, or that of lively energy to the suppleness of Achilles. This being the case, one must see whether, apart from letters,

---

[48] When she later reworked this section of the Preface for a short essay entitled, "Que l'integrité suit la vraye suffisance" [That Integrity Follows True Sufficiency], Marie de Gournay clarified and elaborated her view of Caesar as follows:

> J'excepte Cesar seulement, en toute la vraye classe Philosophique, pour un ame également & profondement forte, instruicte & perduë: Encore doit-on considerer, qu'il n'estoit perdu ny méchant, qu'aux choses où le rapide cours de son ambition l'entraisnoit comme forcé: tres-bon par tout ailleurs.
>
> [I except only Caesar in the whole class of true philosophers, as a soul equally and profoundly strong, learned, and lost: still, one must consider that he was not lost or wicked except in those matters where the rapid course of his ambition drew him along as if compelled: he was superior in all other respects.]
> (*Les Advis, ou, les Presens de la Demoiselle de Gournay 1641*, gen. eds. Jean-Philippe Beaulieu and Hannah Fournier, vol. 1 [Amsterdam and Atlanta, GA: Rodopi, 1997], 253–254)

Montaigne in the *Essais* had been less sparing in depicting Caesar's faults. See the effusive praise of his personal and literary qualities in the veritable "train of the Muses" chronicled in "Des livres [Of Bookes]"—"sauf les fauces couleurs dequoy il veut couvrir sa mauvaise cause et l'ordure de sa pestilente ambition [except the false colours, wherewith he goeth about to cloake his bad cause, and the corruption and filthinesse of his pestilent ambition]" (Villey, ed., 2.10.416[A,C]; trans. Florio, 2: 103). Caesar's duality of character is treated at length in "L'histoire de Spurina [The Historie of Spurina]" (Villey, ed., 2.33.729–733[A]; trans. Florio, 2: 457–462). Cf. also "De Democritus et Heraclitus [Of Democritus and Heraclitus]":

> Cette mesme ame de Caesar, qui se faict voir à ordonner et dresser la bataille de Pharsale, elle se faict aussi voir à dresser des parties oysives et amoureuses. On juge un cheval, non seulement à le voir manier sur une carriere, mais encore à luy voir aller le pas, voire et à le voir en repos à l'estable.
>
> [The very same minde of *Caesar*, we see in directing, marshalling, and setting the battel of *Pharsalia*, is likewise seene to order, dispose, and contrive, idle, trifling and amorous devices. We judge of a horse, not only by seeing him ridden, and cunningly managed, but also by seeing him trot, or pace; yea, if we but looke upon him as he stands in the stable.] (Villey, ed., 1.50.302[A]; trans. Florio, 1: 342)

(The last passage would seem to stand, albeit obliquely, behind Marie de Gournay's collocation, at the opening of the Preface, of Caesar, Pharsalia, and the horse that cannot judge human value—see above, 21.)

[49] Milon of Croton, celebrated Greek athlete (later sixth century B.C.).

exercitation qui peust embesongner toutes entieres l'ame de Socrates et d'Epaminondas[40]. Sera-ce un jugement de procés? Sera-ce l'estude des formes de la cour du Roy de Perse? sera-ce la guerre? sera-ce l'estat? tout cela sont belles choses; mais qui les voudra considerer de pres, trouvera facilement, ce me semble, qu'apres que telles ames auront suffisamment remply tous les devoirs de ces charges, il leur restera des parties vaccantes; et demeureront inoccupez en la guerre, puisqu'Agamemnon la pouvoit soustenir perfaictement[41]; et demeureront inoccupez encore au gouvernement de l'estat, où Priam pouvoit exceller[42].

Nostre peuple a tort[43], qui conçoit un homme vuide d'innocence dés qu'il l'imagine plein de suffisance, et dit que les plus habilles sont les plus meschans, parce qu'il voit les premiers Capitaines et Politiques, ou encore les plus sublins Astrologues, Logiciens, rencontreux, et danceurs, estre ordinairement telz. Nous croions que ces espritz soient les plus haults à cause que nous ne pouvons veoir plus hault qu'eux; ainsi ce Paysan, qui n'avoit jamais veu la mer, cuidoit que chaque riviere fust l'Ocean. C'est planter trop court les bornes de la suffisance. Pour bien fournir à ces functions, il faut voirement estre galand homme; mais pour estre homme parfaict, il faut fournir à plus: la cognoissance du bien et du mal et, contre la tyrannie de la coustume[44], l'art de sentir la juste estendue de nostre clairvoiance, limiter la curiosité, retrencher les vicieux appetiz, faire courber noz forces soubz le joug de la liberté d'autruy,

---

[40] Montaigne met par deux fois Epaminondas «au premier rang des hommes excellens» (II, 36, 756 A; III, 1, 801 B); et l'on sait l'admiration qu'il nourrissait pour Socrate «qui a esté un exemplaire parfaict en toutes grandes qualitez» (III, 12, 1057 B).

[41] Agamemnon, roi d'Argos et de Mycènes, conduisit l'armée grecque contre Troie. Montaigne l'évoque par la voix d'Horace (III, 6, 907 B).

[42] Priam, dernier roi de Troie, célèbre pour sa sagesse politique. Cf. I, 19, 79 A.

[43] Même expression chez Montaigne (III, 6, 900 B).

[44] «C'est à la verité une violente et traistresse maistresse d'escole que la coutume. [...] Elle nous descouvre tantost [bientôt] un furieux et tyrannique visage [...]» (I, 23, 109 A).

which they call philosophy, there would be any activity that could wholly occupy the souls of Socrates and Epaminondas.[50] Will it be a trial-judgment? Will it be the study of the customs of the King of Persia's court? Will it be war? Will it be the state? These are all splendid things; but whoever considers them close up will readily find, it seems to me, that after such spirits have sufficiently fulfilled all the requirements of those tasks, parts of them will still be empty; these will remain unoccupied in war, since Agamemnon could undertake that perfectly,[51] and they will remain unoccupied also in the government of the state, where Priam was able to excel.[52]

Our common people are wrong[53] to fancy a man void of innocence as soon as they imagine him full of sufficiency, and to say that the most able are the most wicked because they see the foremost captains and politicians—or indeed the most adept astrologers, logicians, entertainers, and dancers—ordinarily to be so. We believe that these intellects are the highest because we cannot see above them; just so did the peasant who had never seen the sea think that each river was the ocean. That is to set the bounds of sufficiency at too short a distance. To be equal to these functions, truly it is necessary to be a wise man; but to be a perfect man, one must be capable of more: the knowledge of good and evil and, in despite of the tyranny of custom,[54] the art of sensing the true extent of our discernment,[55] of limiting curiosity, trimming vicious appetites, making our strength bend to the yoke of others' liberty; knowing where

---

[50] Montaigne twice places Epaminondas "au premier rang des hommes excellens [in the first ranke of excellent men]" (Villey, ed., 3.1.801[B] [trans. Florio, 3: 20], recalling 2.36.756[A] [trans. Florio, 2: 488]). The admiration that Montaigne felt for Socrates, who "a esté un exemplaire parfaict en toutes grandes qualitez [hath beene a perfect patterne in all great qualities]" (Villey, ed., 3.12.1057[B]; trans. Florio, 3: 314), is well known.

[51] Agamemnon, king of Argos and Mycenae, led the Greek army against Troy. Montaigne evokes him by way of Horace (Villey, ed., 3.6.907[B]; trans. Florio, 3: 140).

[52] Priam, last king of Troy, celebrated for his political wisdom. Cf. Villey, ed., 1.19.79(A) (trans. Florio, 1: 71).

[53] "Nostre peuple a tort." The same expression occurs in Montaigne, Villey, ed., 3.6.900(B); trans. Florio, 3: 130 ("Our people is to blame").

[54] "Car c'est à la verité une violente et traistresse maistresse d'escole, que la coustume.... elle nous descouvre tantost un furieux et tyrannique visage [For truly, *Custome is a violent and deceiving schoole-mistris*.... it will soone discover a furious and tyrannicall countenance unto us]" (Villey, ed., 1.23.109[A]; trans. Florio, 1: 105).

[55] The following list of practical intellectual attainments is reminiscent of at least one in Montaigne, which similarly begins with, "que c'est que sçavoir et ignorer, qui doit estre le but de l'estude [What it is to know, and not to know (which ought to be the scope of studie)]" (Villey, ed., 1.26.158[A]; trans. Florio, 1: 166).

sçavoir où la vengeance est licite et jusques où, jusques où la gratitude suffit, jusques à quel prix l'approbation publique est achetable, juger des actions humaines, sçavoir quand il est temps de croire et de doubter, aymer et hayr à propos, cognoistre ce qu'autruy nous doit, et nous à luy, et tant d'autres parties en somme requises à conduire la vie selon sa naturelle condition; c'est bien une besongne d'autre et plus grand poix et difficulté. L'oreille n'est qu'une parcelle de nostre estre; mais il seroit tresmal-aisé de me persuader que tous les exploicts de Pyrrhus et d'Alexandre presupposassent autant de vigueur et de sens en leurs autheurs, que son legitime gouvernement seul, à qui le peult avoir[45].

Qui dira combien c'est d'empescher que la calomnie n'entre dedans[46] (soit que certaine lasche et vile malice d'aymer à mesdire luy planisse le chemin, ou l'incapacité de discerner le faux du vray, qui est le plus commun) les faulces nouvelles parfois si vray-semblables et si generallement preschées, les mauvaises suasions, les sottes esperances. Cela n'est pourtant qu'une part de sa charge, et part dont je me taiz, ayant ailleurs dict un mot de la legere creance[47]. Mais l'autre extremité, quoi? Là se giste le desadveu de toutes les vertus qui sont ou hors de nostre veuë, ou hors de nostre experience ou portée: l'injure contre tant de gens d'honneur qui rapportent les histoires, mespris pernicieux d'advertissements, mescreance de miracles, et finallement l'atheisme[48]. C'est grand cas que les hommes ne se puissent sauver d'un vice, sans tomber en son contraire: qu'ils ne cognoissent, dis-je, exemption de la flatterie qu'à jetter des pierres à chacun, guerison de la licence qu'en la servitude, ny de la gourmandise qu'en la famine; et que ceux icy s'estiment plus rusez à cognoistre jusques où va la menterie, s'ils ignorent jusques où la verité peut arriver.

Mon sexe n'a garde de me laisser chommer d'exemples d'avoir veu

---

[45] Non pas Pyrrhus, fils d'Achille, mais le roi d'Epire du même nom qui envahit l'Italie et qu'évoque Montaigne une dizaine de fois dans les *Essais*. Alexandre-le-grand est l'un des «trois [hommes] excellens au dessus de tous les autres» selon Montaigne (II, 36, 754 A).

[46] Le sens continue au-delà de la parenthèse: «dedans [...] les fausses nouvelles».

[47] Allusion probable au *Proumenoir*, œuvre romanesque où l'héroïne, Alinda, est victime de la «legere creance» des hommes.

[48] Montaigne parle de l'«execrable atheisme» où conduisent les «nouvelletez» religieuses qui ébranlent «nostre ancienne creance» (II, 12, 439 A).

vengeance is allowable and how far,⁵⁶ how far gratitude suffices, how high a price must be paid for public approbation; to judge human actions, to know when it is time to believe and to doubt, to love and to hate as is fitting, to recognize what others owe us, and we them; and, in sum, as many other qualities as are required to lead life according to its natural condition: that is indeed a task of other and greater weight and difficulty. The ear is merely one small part of us; but it would be hard indeed to persuade me that all the exploits of Pyrrhus and of Alexander had required as much energy and sense in their authors as does proper self-government alone for one who is capable of it.⁵⁷

Who will say how great a task it is to prevent calumny—whether a certain cowardly and vile pleasure in denigration determines its course or the incapacity to discern false from true, which is more common— from introducing into that ear false reports (sometimes so true-seeming and so widely proclaimed), bad advice, foolish hopes. Still, this is just a part of calumny's assault, and a part about which I remain silent, having elsewhere said something about easy credence.⁵⁸ But what of the other extreme? That way lies the disavowal of all the virtues that are either out of our sight or out of our experience or reach: the attacking of so many honorable persons when they recount events, pernicious contempt of warnings, disbelief in miracles, and finally atheism.⁵⁹ It is a great matter that men cannot save themselves from one vice without falling into its contrary: that they are acquainted, I say, with freedom from flattery only in throwing stones at everyone, with the curing of licence only in the form of servitude and of gluttony only in the form of famine; and that such people consider themselves more clever in being aware of how far lies go, even if they are ignorant of how far the truth may reach.

Thanks to my sex, I hardly lack for occasions of seeing my opinions

---

⁵⁶ This question is a preoccupation of Marie de Gournay, as witnessed by her later essay on the subject (*Les Advis*, ed. Beaulieu and Fournier, 1: 156–172).

⁵⁷ Not Pyrrhus, the son of Achilles, but the king of Epirus of the same name, who invaded Italy and to whom Montaigne refers ten times in the *Essais*. Alexander the Great is one of the "trois [hommes] excellens au dessus de tous les autres [three (men), who have beene excellent above all others]" (Villey, ed., 2.36.751[A]; trans. Florio, 2: 482), according to Montaigne.

⁵⁸ Probable allusion to *Le Proumenoir*, in which the heroine, Alinda, is the victim of "legere creance" [easy credence] with respect to her lover.

⁵⁹ Montaigne speaks of "[l']execrable atheism [execrable Atheisme]" fostered by the religious "novelletez [new fangles]" that shake "nostre ancienne creance [our ancient beleefe]" (Villey, ed., 2.12.439[A]; trans. Florio, 2: 126).

faire le niquet à mes creances et tesmoignages: Si pertinemment ou non, j'ose dire que ce tiltre si bien advoüé de la creature du grand Montaigne, en respondra. De vray, j'en suis là de reputer celuy qui ne sçait croire et decroire à poinct, inhabile à tout autre bien; et ne me fierois à ma notion jour de ma vie, pour certitude qu'il y eust, si je m'estois une fois laissée tromper à elle. Toute franche que je sois de son abus, nul jusques icy ne m'a jamais nyé les choses mesmes que j'ay clairement veues et ouyes, qui ne m'ait jettée en quelque doubte de ma science, et à la queste d'une verification nouvelle. Nous procedons aussi douteusement encore au jugement des consciences du monde. Et s'il se void que nous nous y remettions franchement quand la necessité des occurrences l'ordonne, il ne faut pas qu'on pense, que nous serions deceuz s'il nous en prenoit mal; car avant que d'en venir là nous avons bien preveu qu'il pourroit arriver ainsin: ils ont bien peu nous trahir, non pas nous tromper. Un esprit sage se commet et remet à plusieurs, et se fie de peu de personnes: par ce qu'il est plus d'affaires que de gens d'honneur. Or une chose m'a consolée contre ceux qui se sont mocquez de mes rapports, ou bien à qui mon sexe ou moy sommes autrement en desdain; c'est qu'ils se sont infailliblement declarez des sotz jusques à ce qu'ils ayent prouvé qu'un Montaigne l'estoit, quand il m'estimoit digne, non pas seulement d'une autre estime, mais d'estre admise d'une ame pareille à la sienne en une telle societé qu'estoit la nostre tant que Dieu l'a permis. Mais nous autres, pour estre minces et foiblets, sommes droictement l'entreprise du magnanime courage qui est en ceste espece d'hommes.

Cependant je leur conseille en amye de ne se frotter pas à ceux là qui sont si forts de la plume; il faut tuer telles gens autant que les blesser; ostez la force ou n'attizez pas le courage. Qui leur veut ravir quelque chose, il faut commencer par la teste; car c'est une sottize de les outrager et leur laisser le jardin où croissent les inventions de se venger. Offencer un bel esprit, c'est consciencieusement prouvoir à la repentance de sa faute. On void comme il prit à Minos d'eschauffer la verve de ces causeurs d'Atheniens[49]. Entre nous, femmelettes ne leur serons

---

[49] Minos: roi légendaire de Crète, fils de Jupiter et d'Europe, qui devint après sa mort l'un des juges des Enfers, souvent confondu avec son petit-fils, père d'Ariane et de Phèdre, qui bâtit le Labyrinthe pour le Minotaure et exigea un lourd tribut des Athéniens jusqu'à ce que Thésée ait tué le monstre.

and affirmations held up to ridicule: fittingly or not, I dare to say that the title so widely recognized of "creature of the great Montaigne" will guarantee them. Truly, I am at the point of being considered someone who does not know how to believe and disbelieve as is fitting, incapable of any other good; and I would never in my life pride myself on my intuition, whatever certainty I might have had, if I had let myself be fooled by it a single time. Wholly free though I am of being abused by it, no one so far has ever denied even the things that I have seen and heard without throwing me into doubt about my knowledge, and into a quest for new confirmation. We proceed just as doubtfully also to the judgment of people's consciences. And if it is seen that we return to such judgment boldly when the necessity of circumstances compels it, no one should suppose that we would be surprised if we fell into error; for before coming to it, we have well foreseen that it might turn out this way: they have indeed been able to betray us, not at all to deceive us. A wise mind commits itself to, and consults with, a number and has confidence in few, because there is more business to be done than there are persons of honor. Now one thing has consoled me against those who have mocked my relations with Montaigne, or rather who hold my sex or myself otherwise in disdain; that is, that they have infallibly declared themselves to be fools, insofar as they have proved that a man such as Montaigne was one when he esteemed me worthy, not only of a different estimation, but of being admitted as a soul equal to his own in the sort of association ours was, as long as God permitted it. But our kind, because we are slight and weakling, is fittingly the target of the magnanimous courage that exists in that variety of man.

Nevertheless, I advise them in friendship not to take on those who are so strong with their pens; you have to kill such people as much as wound them; take away their strength or do not inflame their hearts. Whoever wants to snatch something from them had better start with the head; for it is stupidity to outrage them and leave them the garden where vengeful inventions grow. To offend a rare spirit is to ensure, as if by an act of conscience, that one's fault will be repented. We see how it took Minos to kindle the verve of those chattering Athenians.[60]

---

[60] Minos: legendary king of Crete, son of Jupiter and Europa, who after his death became one of the judges of the underworld; often confused with his grandson, the father of Ariadne and Phaedra, who built the labyrinth for the minotaur and demanded a heavy tribute of the Athenians until Theseus slew the monster.

jamais redoutables par là; car ils s'asseurent que la plus haulte suffisance où nous puissions arriver, c'est ressembler le moindre homme. Quoy, s'il n'est pas jusques à nos petits faiseurs d'invectives et de Pasquils[50] qui n'ayent esperé de maistriser le monde par ces armes? Mais ils se trompent; une invective qui ne peut vivre ne peut fraper coup, et ne peut vivre s'elle n'est décochée d'une langue vive et sublime extremement, et ne faict partie d'un bon livre. Il y a moins d'interest qu'ils crachent sur le nom que sur la robbe, et qu'ils parlent que s'ils rottent pres de nous. Que si ce Roy de Crete n'eust point eu d'autres ennemis qu'eux, nous l'eussions bien sauvé d'estre Juge des Lutins et des ombres damnées[51]. Une personne de merite et de prix ne craint point les invectives, sçachant bien qu'un galand et habile homme ne l'attaquera pas, et que, si quelqu'un de ces chetifs brouillons l'entreprend, il luy en prendra comme à l'abeille qui laisse l'aiguillon en la playe; et si fera voir au monde ce dont on pouvoit doubter jusques alors: c'est qu'elle n'est mal voulue que d'un fat. Mais apres tout, comment ne sçauroit une teste forte prendre raison de son ennemy, quand il n'est pas jusques aux molles et delicates filletes qui n'ayent leurs vengeances? et d'autant moins fortes que celles de ces escrivailleurs, qu'elles sont moins en poincte de fourchette et qu'elles sont executées pour satisfaction d'offence, non pour faire gaigner la pepie aux grenouilles à force de crier miracle de leur suffisance, comme ils cuident faire. Et si ce sont vengeances tendres et douces, comme elles.

Escoutez la solemne histoire. Quelques unes en Picardie, piquées contre une autre qui ne faisoit vrayement pas grand compte de si sottes gens que nous, feignans dancer avec elle main à main en pleine

---

[50] Pasquil ou pasquille pour «pasquin», composition satirique injurieuse.
[51] Nouvelle allusion à Minos, juge des enfers; cf. *supra*, note 49.

Between us, we poor little women will never be intimidating to them in this way; for they assure themselves that the height of sufficiency to which we might arrive would be to resemble the least of men. Look if it isn't our little makers of invectives and Pasquils[61] who hope to master the world with these arms! But they are fooling themselves; an invective that cannot live cannot strike home, and it cannot live unless it is shot off in language lively and sublime in the extreme, and does not comprise part of a good book. There is less harm in their spitting on the name than on the dress, and less in speaking than in belching near us. If that King of Crete had had no other enemies but them, we would have saved him from becoming Judge of the Goblins and damned spirits.[62] A person of desert and worth hardly fears invectives, well knowing that a wise and capable man will not attack, and that if one of those feeble muddle-heads takes on the job, he will do it like the bee that leaves its stinger in the wound; and thus he will make the world see what could have been surmised all along: namely, that the person is the target of a poseur. But after all, how would an obstinate fool not know how to get the better of his enemy, when it is even soft and delicate little girls who are out for revenge, and their revenges are all the less strong than those of such scribblers because they are less sharp-pointed and are undertaken to obtain satisfaction for an offense, not to silence the frogs by dint of celebrating their own capacity,[63] as the others think they will do. And so these are revenges tender and sweet, like their authors.

Here is a solemn story for you. Certain girls in Picardy, annoyed with another (who, in truth, did not deem such foolish folks as ourselves to be of much account), pretending to dance with her hand to

---

[61] "Pasquil" or "pasquille" for "pasquin" [pasquinade], an insulting satirical composition.

[62] Another allusion to Minos; see above, n. 60.

[63] Perhaps an allusion to Dionysos' attempt to silence the frogs in the play by Aristophanes. Cf. Erasmus, *Adages*, 3.1.76 (*Collected Works of Erasmus*, vol. 34, trans. and annotated R. A. B. Mynors [Toronto: University of Toronto Press, 1992], 211), on "Minus de istis laboro quam de ranis palustribus / These things trouble me less than frogs in the marsh":

> It will also be used rightly of critics when we wish to say that we emphatically despise their attacks; for frogs may chatter and croak without stopping at the passers-by and endlessly repeat their dreary chorus, "brekekekex koax koax," yet no one is moved in the slightest.

Marie de Gournay would have had access to numerous further expressions, stories, and fables representing frogs as noisy, quarrelsome, envious, nasty, foul, stupid, etc.—see esp. Ovid, *Metamorphoses* 6.312ff.

assemblée, elles se contentent, pour toute la descharge de leur petit cœur, de tenir ferme au premier son des violons pour la laisser esbranler toute seule: si haute toutesfois de taille, de vaillante, belle et favorie maison mais presque deffuncte, qu'on voyoit de bien loing le galbe de sa comedie à un seul personnage; et filles de rire. Pour reprendre donc mon fil des estourdis nieurs, quelqu'un que la fortune a prodigieusement bien traicté, sentant attribuer à certaine personne des advantages, qu'il falloit estre si temerairement sot pour nier ou affermer en vain, qu'un signalé gouvernement d'une de nos villes, un grade honnorable et d'autres actions publiques, disoit au tesmoin, en longues risées, qu'il l'avoit creu parce que celuy dont il estoit mention luy disoit. D'autant qu'il n'en sçavoit rien, il n'estoit pas veritable. Quel pleige de verité qui la touchoit à son experience, ne presumant pas qu'en quelque lieu qu'elle peust estre, elle ne fust ou fort obligée de venir faire hommage, ou fort ambitieuse de se faire cognoistre à luy le premier! Pensez comme il l'eust faict bon croire aux choses doubteuses et cachées, puisqu'il sçavoit nous informer ainsi des communes et vulgaires, et engager une armée en quelque pays soubs le rapport d'un qui pouvoit faucement jurer, non que de ses forces, armes, soldats, munitions, chemins, courage, discipline et conduicte, mais du gouverneur qui le commandoit. Que ne se ramentevoit il combien luy cousta pour un jour la dure creance, lors qu'à faute de vouloir laisser persuader à son outrecuidance, que ses ennemis bien equippez, nobles et vaillans, eussent la hardiesse de l'attaquer, il ruyna son party naguere, dés l'entrée, par sa deffaicte? Ou qu'il ne se ressouvenoit combien ridiculement, au contraire, il laisse à chaque moment, d'une admirable inconstance et bigarrure, mener ses oreilles à tous les contes qu'on luy faict, pourveu qu'ils blessent quelqu'un, et à mille nouvelles mensongeres qu'il croit et trompette luy mesme, et tout justement pour ce notable respect dont il bat les autres, c'est qu'on lui a dict? Celuy qui renomme quelqu'un de croire à cause qu'on luy dict,

hand in the midst of an assembly, were content, for the full discharge of their little hearts, to resolve to leave her all alone, dancing, at the first sound of the violins: yet so tall of stature, and of a valiant, splendid, and favored noble house (though all but extinct), that one saw from afar the shape of the one-character comedy she was acting—and the girls broke into laughter.[64] To return, then, to my theme of light-headed scorners, someone whom fortune had treated prodigiously well, perceiving that a certain person was being endowed with advantages which one would have had to be so recklessly foolish to deny or dismiss as empty, such as an important governorship of one of our towns, an honorable rank, and other forms of public recognition, said to a witness, in a long mocking speech, that he had believed it because the man in question told him so. Insofar as he knew nothing about it, it was not true. What a pledge of Truth it is to test her on the basis of one's experience, not presuming that, in whatever place she may be, she is either stringently obliged to come and pay homage or greatly ambitious to make herself known to him first! Think how, since he knew how to inform us about common and vulgar things in this way, he would have been made to believe in doubtful and hidden ones and to engage an army in some country on the report of anyone able to swear falsely, not just as to its strength, arms, soldiers, munitions, routes, courage, discipline, and conduct, but about the governor who commanded him. Does he not remember how much his difficult credence recently cost him in a single day, when, rather than let his overweening pride be persuaded that his enemies, well equipped, noble, and valiant, would have the boldness to attack him, he ruined his party at the outset by his defeat? Or does he not recall how ridiculously, on the other hand, he allows his ears to be led at every moment, with wonderful inconstancy and variation, by all the tales he is told, provided that they injure someone, and by a thousand false reports that he credits and trumpets himself, and precisely because of that notable respect with which he exceeds others—or so they told him? He who celebrates someone for believing because he has been told, if he is not

---

[64] Cathleen M. Bauschatz temptingly reads this incident as a "pathetic example of a painful girlhood experience" distanced by third-person narration; if so, there is a further distancing effect in "as ourselves" ["que nous"]. See Bauschatz's essay, "Imitation, Writing, and Self-Study in Marie de Gournay's 1595 'Préface' to Montaigne's *Essais*," in *Contending Kingdoms: Historical, Psychological, and Feminist Approaches to the Literature of Sixteenth-Century England and France*, ed. Marie-Rose Logan and Peter L. Rudnytsky (Detroit, MI: Wayne State University Press, 1991), 363 n. 24.

s'il ne le cognoist un gros et lourd animal, il l'est luy mesme en ce qu'il ne sçait pas discerner combien ce vice là pourroit mal compatir avec une once de sens.

Je voudrois que nous n'eussions pas veu des gens de profession plus serieuse, gastez de pareil meslange de ces pernicieuses humeurs. Apres qu'ils auront creu dix fois à tort et presché que telle ou telle ville seront prises, ils cuident bien r'allier leur creance à la gravité, s'ils se mocquent de quelque histoire, ny merveilleuse ny rare, que quelqu'un d'entre nous chetifs rapportera peut estre de cinquante lieues: comme si l'on se guerissoit d'estre un fat, se rendant injurieux, et comme s'il y avoit moings d'ineptie à suivre une fauce dissuasion qu'une suasion faulce, et à se croire legerement soy-mesme qu'autruy. Certes, quand nous serions si bestes que le reproche qu'on feroit à noz contes se trouvast vray, si ne seroit pas nostre sottise de l'avoir creu, par ce que nous l'aurions ouy dire, plus grande que la leur, de l'avoir nié parce qu'ilz ne le sçavoient pas. Y a il tant d'affaires à recevoir de cette sorte les nouvelles obscures et les estranges, et les monstreuses encores? Je ne rejette pas cela comme faux, mais j'y refuse ma creance comme à chose non prouvée[52].

Or revenons, pour dire que la plus generalle censure qu'on face de nostre livre, c'est que, d'une entreprise particuliere à luy, son autheur s'y depeint[53]. Les belles choses qu'il dict sur ce point! Si je pouvois estre induitte à vouloir respecter la haine que le peuple porte à la particularité, si grande qu'il n'adore jamais Dieu mesme que soubz sa forme, je luy pourrois demander que faisoient autre chose ces anciens qui descrivoient leurs propres gestes jusques aux moindres; mais je ne me soucie gueres de ce reproche: il n'appartient qu'à ceux qui mescognoissent le monde, à craindre de luy dissembler, ou bien à ceux qui le veulent flatter et chattouiller de leur perte. Quoy, si nous arrivions en ces nations où, selon Pline, on ne vivoit que d'odeur, ce seroit donc folie de

---

[52] On retrouve ici les marques du pyrrhonisme montaignien. Cf. II, 12, *passim*.
[53] Réponse aux critiques de l'auto-portrait. On pense déjà à Pascal dénonçant le «sot projet» que Montaigne a eu de se peindre. *Pensées, II, 62.*

aware that such a person is a gross and dull animal, is one himself, in that he cannot discern to what extent that vice is poorly compatible with an ounce of sense.

I wish that we had not seen some people who profess themselves more serious spoiled by a similar mixture of these pernicious humors. After they have believed wrongly ten times and proclaimed that this or that town has been taken, they think it better to realign their credence with gravity, if it means mocking some story, neither marvelous nor uncommon, that one of us weaklings brings back from perhaps fifty leagues: as if one were curing oneself of pretentious stupidity by making oneself insulting, and as if there were less ineptitude in a false dissuasion than in a false persuasion, and in believing oneself readily rather than others. Certainly, when we should be so stupid that the reproach that our stories incur would prove true, our folly for having believed it because we heard it said would still not be greater than theirs for having denied it because they did not know it. Are there such great difficulties in receiving in this manner obscure and strange tidings, and even monstrous ones? I do not reject such a thing as false, but I refuse it my belief as something not proven.[65]

Now, to get back to the point, let us say that the most general censure with which our book is confronted is that, in an undertaking peculiarly his own, its author depicts himself in it.[66] The beautiful things that he says on this point! If I could be induced willingly to respect the hate that the ordinary sort of people bear towards particularities of character, so great that they never adore even God except in outward form, I could ask them what else those ancients were doing who described their own actions down to the least; but I am hardly troubled by this reproach: it is the part only of those who do not know the world well to fear not to resemble it, or of those who wish to flatter and tickle it, to their own loss. So, if we arrived amongst those nations where, according to Pliny, one lives only by smell, it would then be

---

[65] One finds here the signs of Montaigne's Pyrrhonism. Cf. Villey, ed., 2.12 *passim*.

[66] A response to criticisms of the self-portrait. This is to anticipate Blaise Pascal, who would denounce Montaigne's "sot projet"—the "folly of trying to paint his own portrait" (*Pascal's Pensées*, trans. and ed. H. F. Stewart [London: Routledge and Kegan Paul, 1950], 16–17 [No. 39]).

manger⁵⁴. Apres tout, messieurs de Montluc et de la Noue se sont ilz pas de nostre aage descritz et representez eux mesmes aussi, par le registre de leurs actions, dont ilz ont faict present à leur pays⁵⁵? remerciables en cela deux fois: l'une, de leur labeur; l'autre, de l'avoir appliqué sur tel subject; car ilz n'eussent peu rien escrire de plus vray que ce qu'ilz avoient faict eux mesmes, ny rien de plus utile que ce qu'ilz avoient si bien faict. Je ne parle pas de la cause des armes de ce dernier⁵⁶, ains seulement de la valeur et suffisance d'icelles. S'il leur semble qu'il soit bien loisible de produire au jour ces actions publiques et non les privées, certes, outre que ces Seigneurs font cela mesme, descrivans jusques à leurs songes, ilz n'entendent pas que valent ny les publiques ny les domestiques, ny que le publicq mesme n'est faict que pour le particulier⁵⁷. Il leur semble que la science de vivre soit si facile, qu'on fait une sottise quand on daigne publier sa pratique. Car mesme ilz sentent bien que leurs enfans ne sçauroient ny dancer, ny picquer chevaux, ny trencher à table, ny saluer, qui ne leur apprend⁵⁸; mais, quant à cet art, ilz ne l'y trouverent jamais à dire⁵⁹. Certes il est trop plus aisé de vaincre que de vivre, et plus de triumphans que de sages.

Mon Pere a cuydé ne te pouvoir rien mieux apprendre que la cognoissance et l'usage de toy-mesme: tantost par raisons, tantost par

---

⁵⁴ Montaigne attribue à Plutarque et non à Pline cette observation sur «des hommes sans bouche, se nourrissans de la senteur de certaines odeurs» (II, 12, 525 A); mais il avait mentionné le nom de Pline à la ligne précédente dans l'édition de 1580.

⁵⁵ Blaise de Montluc (1502-1577) dans ses célèbres *Commentaires,* Bordeaux, 1592, et François de La Noue, dit Bras de Fer (1531-1591), dans ses *Discours politiques et militaires,* Bâle, 1587. Montaigne les cite tous les deux dans les *Essais* (II, 8, 395 A et II, 17, 661 C).

⁵⁶ La Noue avait embrassé la cause des Protestants et combattit aux côtés d'Henri IV à Ivry pour vaincre les Ligueurs (1590).

⁵⁷ «Est-ce raison que, si *particulier* en usage [moi qui mène une vie si privée], je pretende me rendre *public* en cognoissance [je prétende me faire connaître de tout le monde]?» (III, 2, 805 B).

⁵⁸ Si on ne leur apprend.

⁵⁹ Comprendre: Mais quant à l'art de vivre, ils n'ont jamais pensé qu'il leur faisait défaut.

madness to eat.⁶⁷ After all, have not Messieurs Montluc and La Noue in our own time described and represented themselves also by the record of their actions, which they have presented to their country?⁶⁸ They are worthy to be thanked twice for this: once, for their effort; secondly, for having applied it to this subject; for they would not have been able to write anything more true than what they had done themselves, nor anything more useful than that which they have done so well. (I speak not of the cause for which the latter took up arms,⁶⁹ but only of his merit and capacity in wielding them.) If it seems to them that it is indeed praiseworthy to bring to light these public actions and not private ones, certainly (apart from the fact that these Lords do the very thing, describing even their dreams), they do not understand the value of either the public or the domestic, nor that the public itself is not undertaken except for the sake of the private.⁷⁰ It seems to them that the science of living is so easy that one is foolish in deigning to publish the practice of it. For even they sense well that their children would not know how either to dance, to spur a horse, to carve at table, or to make a salutation, if one did not teach them; but as for that art,⁷¹ they never find anything to say. Certainly, it is too much easier to vanquish than to live, and there are more conquerors than sages.

My Father believed that he could not teach you anything better than how to know and employ yourself—sometimes by reasoning things out,

---

⁶⁷ Montaigne attributes to Plutarch, not to Pliny, this observation on "des hommes sans bouche, se nourrissans de la senteur de certaines odeurs [men without mouthes, and who live only by the smell of certaine sweet odours]" (Villey, ed., 2.12.525[A]; trans. Florio, 2: 231), but he had mentioned the name of Pliny in the preceding line in the edition of 1580.

⁶⁸ Blaise de Montluc (1502-1577) in his celebrated *Commentaires* (Bordeaux: S. Millanges, 1592) and François de La Noue, known as Bras de Fer (Iron Arm) (1531-1591), in his *Discours politiques et militaires* (Basel: F. Forest, 1587). Montaigne cites both of them in the *Essais* (Villey, ed., 2.8.395[A] and 2.17.661[C]; trans. Florio, 2: 79 and 389). The first of these instances focuses the issue of public versus private life by way of Montluc's lament that he never showed his affection for his son before the latter was killed in battle; the second reference, which immediately precedes Montaigne's tribute to Marie de Gournay herself, praises La Noue for his "constante bonté, douceur de moeurs et facilité consciencieuse [constant goodnes, . . . mildnes in behaviour, and conscionable facility]" despite his training and excellence in arms.

⁶⁹ La Noue had embraced the cause of the Protestants and fought at the side of Henri IV at Ivry to defeat the Leaguers (1590).

⁷⁰ Cf. the *Essais*: "Mais est-ce raison que, si particulier en usage, je pretende me rendre public en cognoissance? [But is it reason, that being so private in use, I should pretend to make my selfe publike in knowledge?]" (Villey, ed., 3.2.805[B]; trans. Florio, 3: 24).

⁷¹ I.e., the "science of living."

espreuve⁶⁰. Si sa peinture est vicieuse ou fauce, plainds toy de luy; s'elle est bonne et vraye, remercie-le de n'avoir voulu refuser à ta discipline le poinct plus instructif de tous, c'est l'exemple⁶¹; et le plus bel exemple de l'Europe, c'estoit sa vie. Et, en ce que ses ennemis le blasment qu'il y ait rapporté jusques aux moindres particularitez de son institution, c'est de cela mesme qu'ils le doibvent louër; car il n'estoit point avant luy de maistre de ceste leçon, si necessaire neantmoings au service de la vie: tant parce que les grandes choses deppendent des petites, que d'autant aussi que la vie mesme n'est qu'une contexture de punctilles. Voyez le conseil des Roys assemblé si souvent sur la preseance de deux femmes. Les autres autheurs ont eu tort de ne s'arrester à nous instruire en des actions, pour petites qu'elles fussent, où plusieurs pouvoient faillir et que nul ne pouvoit eviter⁶². Et n'est rien d'important qui soit petit: il pese assez, s'il touche. Il a vrayement eu raison de montrer comme il se gouvernoit en l'amour, au deuiz, à la table, voire à la garderobe: puis que tant d'hommes se sont perdus pour ne sçavoir se comporter à la table, au deuis, en l'amour et en la garderobe encore. Son exemple te semble-il bon? rends graces à la fortune qu'il soit tombé devant tes yeux; te semble-il mauvais? ne crains pas aussi que beaucoup de peuple soit pour le suyvre. Quoy? tu le blasmes d'avoir parlé de soy mesme, et ne le louës de n'avoir rien faict qu'il n'ait osé dire, ny de la plus meritoire verité de toutes, celle qu'on dit de soy. C'est la pitié que

---

⁶⁰ Montaigne cite le fameux aphorisme gravé au tympan du temple de Delphes: «Que vous cognoissiez ce qui est à vous, suivant l'inscription Delphique» (II, 8, 398 C). Voir aussi III, 9, 1001 B et III, 13, 1075 B.

⁶¹ Montaigne croit à la fois à la nécessité (III, 2, 805 B) et aux limites de l'exemple: «tout exemple cloche» (III, 13, 1070 B).

⁶² L'opposition aux «autres autheurs» est déjà chez Montaigne (III, 2, 804 B et 805 C).

sometimes by putting them to the proof.⁷² If his depiction is vicious or false, you may complain; if it is good and true, thank him for not having wished to refuse your attaining of right conduct the most instructive point of all, that is, example;⁷³ and the most sublime example in Europe was his life. And, in the very respect that his enemies blame him—that he has reported the particulars of his education down to the least detail—they ought to be praising him; for there is no better master of this lesson, so necessary though it is to the business of life: as much because the great things depend on the small ones as, in addition, because life itself is merely a composite of little details. Consider the council of kings assembled so often to consider the precedence of two women.⁷⁴ Other authors have been wrong to stop short of instructing us in actions, however slight, in which many might have failed and which no one could avoid.⁷⁵ And there is nothing important that is slight: it has its weight, if it touches us. He was indeed right to show how he conducted himself in love, in mourning, indeed in his wardrobe, since so many men have been lost for not knowing how to behave at table, in mourning, in love, and even in the wardrobe.⁷⁶ Does his example seem good to you?—give thanks to fortune that it came before your eyes; does it seem bad?—do not be so fearful that many people are likely to follow it. Really, do you blame him for having spoken of himself, and not praise him for having done nothing that he dared not speak about, even with regard to the most admirable truth of all—that which one says of oneself? It is a pity that those who criticize him for having

---

⁷² Montaigne cites the famous aphorism (cf. above, n. 8) engraved on the tympanum of the temple of Delphi: "que vous cognoissiez ce qui est à vous, suivant l'inscription Delphique [to know ... what is yours, according to the *Delphike* inscription]" (Villey, ed., 2.8.398[C]; trans. Florio, 2: 83). See also 3.9.1001(B) (trans. Florio, 3: 252) and 3.13.1075(B) (trans. Florio, 3: 334). Cf. further the opening of 3.13: "Il n'est desir plus naturel que le desir de connoissance. Nous essayons tous les moyens qui nous y peuvent mener. Quand la raison nous faut, nous y employons l'experience ... [There is no desire more naturall, then that of knowledge. We attempt all meanes that may bring us unto it. When reason failes us, we employ experience.]" (Villey, ed., 3.13.1065[B]; trans. Florio, 3: 322).

⁷³ Montaigne believes at once in the necessity (Villey, ed., 3.2.805[B]; trans. Florio, 3: 23-24) and in the limitations of example: "tout exemple cloche [Every example limpeth]" (Villey, ed., 3.13.1070[B]; trans. Florio, 3: 328).

⁷⁴ This sounds like a specific allusion, which, however, we have not been able to trace.

⁷⁵ The opposition to "other authors" is already in Montaigne (Villey, ed., 3.2.804[B] and 805[C]; trans. Florio, 3: 23-24).

⁷⁶ "Wardrobe," like Marie de Gournay's "garderobe," could in this period mean "privy" (*OED*). This is the common sense of "garderobe" in the *Essais*—see, e.g., Villey, ed., 1.32.216(A) and 3.10.1012(B) (trans. Florio, 1: 231 and 3: 263).

ceux qui le pinsent de nous avoir donné sa peincture, osent, encore moins qu'ils ne veulent, en faire ainsi de la leur; et qu'ils declarassent avoir plus de sottise que d'immodestie, s'ils dessignoient de se monstrer. Je ne sçay s'il a raison de se produire nud devant le peuple: mais je sçay bien que nul ne peut avoir bonne grace à l'en accuser, sauf celuy là, qui perd de la gloire à s'abstenir d'en faire autant. Tu prends, au reste, singulier plaisir qu'on te face voir un grand chef d'armée et d'estat; il faut estre honneste homme avant que d'estre cela perfaictement: nos *Essais* enseignent à le devenir; il faut passer par leur estamine, qui ne veut monter là haut sans jambes[63]. Particulierement quelle escole de guerre et d'estat est-ce que ce livre? En fin le nœud de nostre querelle, c'est, que Xenophon se peinct avec la guerre et l'estat, et Montaigne peinct la guerre et l'estat avec luy[64].

Il est une autre sorte d'impertinens juges des *Essais* entre ceux mesmes qui les ayment; ce sont les mediocres loüeurs. Quiconque dit de Scipion que c'est un gentil Capitaine, et de Socrates, un galand homme, leur faict plus de tort que tel qui totalement ne parle point d'eux, à cause que, si on ne leur donne tout, on leur oste tout. Vous ne sçauriez louer telles gens en les mesurant. On peut autant pecher à la quantité qu'à la qualité des tesmoignages. L'excellence fuit tous limites, non que limites semblables; la seule gloire la borne. Et j'ose dire que ceux qui blasment les *Essays,* et ceux là qui ne les font seulement que louer, les

---

[63] «Qu'il [le précepteur] lui [l'enfant] face tout passer par l'estamine [...]» (I, 26, 151 A).

[64] Montaigne met Xénophon au nombre de ces «hommes rares et fameux» qui ont droit de «se servir de soy pour subject à escrire» (II, 18, 663 A).

given us his portrait do not wish, much less dare, to do the same with their own, and that they would have declared themselves to possess more stupidity than immodesty had they intended to show themselves. I do not know if he is right to produce himself naked before the people; but I well know that no one can justly denounce him for it, except someone who diminishes his own glory in refusing to do as much. You take singular pleasure, moreover, when one displays for you a great leader of an army and a state; one must be an honorable man before one can be that perfectly: our *Essays* teach how to become one; one must pass through their sieve,[77] if one does not wish to climb such a height without legs.[78] What school of war and statecraft, in particular, is that book? In the end, the nub of our quarrel is that Xenophon paints himself by means of war and statecraft, and Montaigne paints war and statecraft together with himself.[79]

There is another sort of impertinent judge of the *Essays* even amongst those who like them: these are the faint praisers. Whoever says of Scipio that he is a noble captain and of Socrates that he is a wise man does them more wrong than one who does not speak of them at all, given that, if one does not grant them all, one deprives them of all. You cannot praise such persons and measure them at the same time. One may as readily err in the quantity as in the quality of the reports. Excellence exceeds all limits, not only such limits; glory itself alone bounds it. And I dare say that those who blame the *Essays* and those who merely praise

---

[77] Cf. the *Essais* (of teacher and pupil): "Qu'il luy face tout passer par l'estamine [I would have him make his scholler narrowly to sift all things with discretion]" (Villey, ed., 1.26.151[A]; trans. Florio, 1: 156).

[78] Perhaps influenced by the following passage at the conclusion of the "Apologie de Raimond Sebond [An Apologie of *Raymond Sebond*]": "... d'esperer enjamber plus que de l'estanduë de nos jambes, cela est impossible et monstrueux. Ny que l'homme se monte au dessus de soy et de l'humanité.... Il s'eslevera si Dieu lui preste extraordinairement la main [... to hope to straddle more then our legs length; is impossible and monstrous: nor that man should mount over and above himselfe or humanity.... He shall raise himselfe up, if it please God extraordinarily to lend him his helping hand]" (Villey, ed., 2.12.604[A]; trans. Florio, 2: 325–326). Cf. also, from the very end of the *Essais*: "Nous cherchons d'autres conditions, pour n'entendre l'usage des nostres, et sortons hors de nous, pour ne sçavoir quel il y fait. Si avons nous beau monter sur des eschasses, car sur des eschasses encores faut-il marcher de nos jambes [We seeke for other conditions because we understand not the use of ours: and goe out of our selves, forsomuch as we know not what abiding there is. *Wee may long enough get upon stilts, for be wee upon them, yet must we goe with our owne legges*]" (Villey, ed., 3.13.1115[B,C]; trans. Florio, 3: 386).

[79] Montaigne places Xenophon amongst those "hommes rares et fameux [rare and famous men]" who have the right to "se servir de soy pour subject à escrire [to make himselfe a subject to write of]" (Villey, ed., 2.18.663[A]; trans. Florio, 2: 390).

mescognoissent esgallement. La loüange est pour d'autres, l'admiration pour eux. Combien j'aye veu peu de Syndics capables de leur faict, c'est à moy de le dire. Parmy ceux que je n'ay pas veuz, je croy qu'il en soit aussi peu; et ma raison, c'est que si quelqu'un les cognoist bien à poinct, il en crie merveille si haut qu'il seroit à mon advis difficile que je ne l'ouysse. Noz gens pensent bien sauver l'honneur de leur jugement quand ils disent: «C'est un gentil ouvrage»: car voyla leur gentil eloge plus ordinaire; ou, «Cest un bel œuvre»: un enfant de huict années en diroit bien autant. Je leur demande par où et jusques où beau, par où il esgalle les premiers des anciens, par où il les passe, et en quelle part ils sont beaux, sinon en celle où ils le ressemblent. Je veux sçavoir quelle force a surmonté la sienne, quels argumens, quelles raisons, quel jugement s'esgalle au sien ou, pour le moings, s'est jamais osé si plainement esprouver, s'est offert si à nud, et nous a jamais laissé si peu à doubter de sa mesure et si peu à desirer de luy. Je laisse à part sa grace et son elegance qui peuvent à l'adventure avoir plus de juges. Or, nonobstant, s'il eust esté produit du temps de ces grands anciens, encore eust on peu s'excuser de l'admirer moings sur ce qu'il eust eu son pareil. Mais en la maigreur des esprits de nostre aage, et en un aage eslongné de 14. ou 15. cens ans du dernier livre qui se venteroit de luy tenir contre-carre, je me puis certainement respondre qu'il eust ravy, comme moy, tous ceux qui l'eussent sçeu cognoistre[65].

Quoy? si nous oyons parler d'un animal monstreux, d'un homme plus hault ou plus petit que l'ordinaire, voire de je ne sçay quel bateleur qui fera des singeries nouvelles ou sauts bigerres, chacun, et les plus huppez, y courent comme au feu; et ceux qui reviendront d'un tel spectacle ne rencontrent en leur chemin nul de leurs cognoissans ny de leurs voisins qu'ils n'en abreuvent de fil en esguille; et si pensent estre obligez, par devoir d'amitié, de le mander aux absens, cuydans que si

---

[65] Marie de Gournay prête ici à Montaigne les qualités que celui-ci attribuait à La Boétie, en particulier sa ressemblance avec les «grands anciens». Cf. *Essais* I, 28: La Boétie arrivait «bien pres de l'honneur de l'antiquité» (184 A). «Il avoit son esprit moulé au patron d'autres siecles que ceux-cy» (194 A).

them equally misrecognize them. Praise belongs elsewhere; what becomes them is admiration.[80] How few critics I have seen capable of appreciating their achievement is for me to say. Amongst those whom I have not seen, I believe that there are just as few; and my reason is that if anyone knows them thoroughly, he cries out his admiration so loudly that it would be difficult for me, I take it, not to hear him. These sorts of people suppose that they are preserving the honor of their judgment when they say, "It's a nice work" (for that is ordinarily their nicest compliment), or, "It's a beautiful work." An eight-year-old child would say just as much. I ask them where and to what degree it is beautiful, where it equals the foremost works of the ancients, where it surpasses them, and in what parts the latter are beautiful, besides those where they resemble it. I wish to know: what force has exceeded his, what arguments, what reasons? what judgment is equal to his, or, at least, has ever dared so fully to hazard itself, has offered itself so nakedly, and has ever left us so little room to doubt its greatness and so little to desire of it? I put aside its grace and elegance, which may perhaps have more judges. Now, nevertheless, if it had been produced in the time of those great ancients, one might still have excused oneself for admiring it less on the grounds that it would have had its equal. But in the thinness of the spirits of our age, and in an age distant by fourteen or fifteen hundred years from the last book that would have boasted of being its equivalent, I can certainly answer that it would have ravished, as it did me, all those who knew how to make its acquaintance.[81]

What? if we hear tell of a monstrous animal, of a man taller or shorter than ordinary, indeed, of some entertainer or other who will do new apish tricks or bizarre leaps, everyone, including the most upper of the upper crust, rush there as if to a fire; and those on their way back from such a show encounter no one in their path amongst their acquaintance or neighbors whom they do not cram with a blow-by-blow account of it; and they actually think themselves obliged by the duty of

---

[80] "La loüange est pour d'autres, l'admiration pour eux." We have preserved the ambiguity existing in the French as to whether "they" ("eux") are the would-be critics or the *Essais* themselves.

[81] Marie de Gournay here assigns to Montaigne the qualities that he attributed to La Boétie, in particular his resemblance to the "grands anciens." According to the *Essais*, La Boétie came "bien pres de l'honneur de l'antiquité [very neerely . . . (to) the honour of antiquity]" (Villey, ed., 1.28.184[A]; trans. Florio, 1: 196), and "Il avoit son esprit moulé au patron d'autres siecles que ceux-cy [His minde was modelled to the patterne of other best ages]" (Villey, ed., 1.28.194[A]; trans. Florio, 1: 209).

quelqu'un perdoit sa part de la merveille, il seroit à plaindre jaçoit qu'il se voye tous les jours des choses semblables. Et l'on nous voudroit faire accroire que, s'ils avoyent gousté ce livre, ils ne seroyent pas accouruz de toutes parts veoir et practiquer l'ame qui le conceut: ame, dis-je, qu'on ne veoit, ny souvent, ny rarement, mais unique depuis tant de siecles; ou, pour le moins, que ceux qui n'auroient peu luy venir toucher en la main, n'eussent pas cherché des inventions de le louer et proclamer, aussi hors d'exemple que son merite l'estoit. Lipsius l'a il cognu seulement un moys qu'on n'ait ouy la voix de son admiration retentir par toute l'Europe[66]? Il sçavoit bien aussi qu'il alloit non seullement de la conscience à rendre à quelqu'un moins de loüange qu'il n'appartient, mais aussi de l'honneur, et que celuy qui lit un livre se donne à l'espreuve plus qu'il ne l'y met.

La vraye touche des esprits c'est l'examen d'un œuvre nouveau. C'est pourquoy je veux tant de mal aux desrobeurs et frippeurs de livres; car s'il s'eslevoit quelque bon autheur moderne, le frequent exemple de ces larrons faisant justement doubter qu'il teint sa beauté d'autruy, et nostre ignorance à nous autres empeschant de nous en esclaircir, il adviendroit qu'à faulte d'applaudir à son merite nous nous declarerions treslourdement des bestes. Celuy qui veoit un ouvrage et n'honnore l'autheur, cet autheur est un fat, ou luy mesme. Les *Essays* sont eschappez à ce soupçon; il est facile à veoir qu'ils sont tout d'une main: livre d'un air nouveau. Tous autres, et les anciens encore, ont l'exercice de l'esprit pour fin, du jugement par accident; il a pour dessein, au rebours, l'escrime du jugement et, par rencontre, de l'esprit, fleau perpetuel des erreurs communes. Les autres enseignent la sapience, il desenseigne la sottise. Et a bien eu raison de vouloir vuider l'ordure hors du vaze, avant que d'y verser l'eau de nafe. Il evente cent mines nouvelles: mais combien inventables? Il est bien certain que jamais homme ne dit ny considera ce que cestuy-cy a dit et consideré sur les actions et passions humaines; mais il

---

[66] Lipsius: Juste Lipse. Cf. *supra*, note 9. Dans une lettre publique il avait appelé Montaigne «le Thalès français». Cf. *supra*, note 12.

friendship to communicate it to those who were not there, believing that if anyone missed his portion of the miracle, he would have reason to complain, although similar things are seen every day. And we are expected to believe that, if they had sampled this book, they would not have run from every direction to see and have first-hand experience of the soul that conceived it: a soul, I say, such as one sees neither often nor rarely, but which has been without parallel for so many centuries; or that, at least, those who could not have come to touch him by the hand would not have sought out inventions as unparalleled as his merit for praising and proclaiming him. Hadn't Lipsius known him for but a month when one heard the voice of his admiration resounding all through Europe?[82] He too knew well that it infringed not only conscience but also honor to render someone less praise than belonged to him, and that he who reads a book puts himself to the test more than he tests it.

The true touchstone of intellects is the examination of a new work. This is why I wish so much ill to plunderers and filchers of books; for if there should arise some good modern author, given that the frequent example of these thieves rightly makes us doubt whether he takes his luster from others and our own ignorance prevents us from clearing up the question, the result would be that, instead of applauding his merit, we would clumsily declare our own stupidity. He who sees a work and does not honor the author—either the author is a poseur, or he himself. The *Essays* have escaped this suspicion; it is easy to see that they are entirely by one hand: it has the *feel* of a new book. All others, and even the ancients, have as their goal the exercise of intellect; that of judgment is a matter of chance. He, on the contrary, has as his design the fencing that sharpens judgment, and perhaps intellect, the perpetual scourge of common errors. The others teach wisdom; he *un*-teaches foolishness. And he had good reason to want to empty the rubbish out of the vase before pouring in the orange-blossom water. He brings to light a hundred new things from underground; but how many could be lighted on?[83] It is certain enough that never has a man said or considered what he has said and considered regarding human actions and passions; but it

---

[82] On Justus Lipsius, see above, n. 11.

[83] Our translation, at the risk of a certain clumsiness, attempts to convey Marie de Gournay's play on words in the original sentence: "Il evente [exposes to the air] cent mines nouvelles: mais combien inventables [discoverable]?" "Éventer la mine" is an expression meaning "discover the secret."

n'est pas certain si jamais homme, luy hors, l'eust peu dire et considerer. Jamais ces livres antiques, pour grands qu'ils fussent, ne sçeurent espuiser les sources de l'esprit; cestuy-cy, luy seul, semble avoir espuisé celles du jugement. Il a tant jugé qu'il ne reste plus que juger apres.

Et parce que mon ame n'a de sa part autre maniement que celuy de juger et raisonner de ceste sorte, la nature m'ayant faict tant d'honneur que, sauf le plus et le moings, j'estois toute semblable à mon Pere, je ne puis faire un pas, soit escrivant ou parlant, que je ne me trouve sur ses traces; et croy qu'on cuide souvent que je l'usurpe. Et le seul contentement que j'euz oncques de moy-mesme, c'est d'avoir rencontré plusieurs choses parmy les dernieres additions que tu verras en ce volume, lesquelles j'avois imaginées toutes pareilles, avant que les avoir veues. Ce livre est en fin le throsne judicial de la raison ou, plus proprement, son ame; l'hellebore de la folie humaine; le hors de page des esprits; la resurrection de la verité; le parfaict en soy-mesme et la perfection des autres[67]. Et qui cherchera l'interpretation de ce mot regarde quel service il leur faict souvent en les anatomisant. Or, pour revenir, si les personnages dont je parlois n'agueres n'ont recherché ceste grande ame, c'est, à l'adventure, pour veriffier en eux la proposition philosophique: que le sage se contente de luy mesme. Vrayment ouy, pourveu qu'il n'y eust qu'eux au monde. Mon Pere me voulant un jour faire desplaisir, me dit, qu'il estimoit qu'il y eust trente hommes en nostre grande ville, où lors il estoit, aussi forts de teste que luy. L'un de mes argumens à le desdire fut que s'il y en eust eu quelqu'un, il feust venu le bien vienner et, me plaist d'adjouster, l'idolastrer; et que tant de gens l'accueilloient pour un homme de bonne maison, de credit et de qualité: nul, pour Montaigne.

Allez vous y fier que les humeurs de nostre siecle sont grandement en queste d'esprits qui pensent que leur recherche et leur accointance, voire une simple frequentation, leur faict injure, s'ils ne l'attachent aux qualitez. Et si Socrates renaissoit, un gros monsieur auroit honte de faire

---

[67] Dans une lettre à Juste Lipse, Marie de Gournay avait déjà donné une version de ce passage: «c'est le bréviaire des demi-dieux, le contre-poison d'erreur, le hors de page des âmes, la resurrection de la verité, l'hellébore du sens humain et l'esprit de la raison». *Lettre du 25 avril 1593*, Dezon-Jones, p. 188.

is not certain if any man, apart from him, would have been able to say and consider it. Never could those ancient books, as great as they were, exhaust the well-springs of the intellect; this one seems to have exhausted, all by itself, those of judgment. He has done so much judging that there is nothing left but to judge after him.

And because my soul, for its part, has no other way of managing but to judge and reason in this way, nature having done me so much honor that, except in the greatest and the least respects, I was wholly like my Father, I cannot take a step, whether in writing or speaking, without finding myself in his footsteps; and I believe that I am often supposed to usurp him. And the only time that I have ever been content with myself was when, amongst the recent additions you will see in this volume, I encountered a number of things that I had imagined in just the same way before seeing them. This book is, in the end, the judicial throne of reason or, more fittingly, its soul; hellebore for the madness of humanity; the unwritten language of intellects; the resurrection of truth; perfection in itself and the means of perfecting others.[84] And whoever seeks to know what perfection means will see what a service he often does them by anatomizing them. Now, to get back to my theme, if persons of the kind I have been speaking of have scarcely sought out this great soul, that serves, perhaps, to verify in them the philosophical proposition that the wise man is satisfied with himself. Yes, truly, if there were nobody besides themselves in the world. My Father, wishing to displease me one day, told me he judged that there were thirty men in our great city, where he was at that time, with as powerful an intellect as himself. One of my arguments in countering this was that if there had been one, he would have come to greet him and, I was fain to add, idolize him; and that so many people received him for being a man of good family, of credit, and of noble birth: none for being Montaigne.

Depend on it: the humors of our time are greatly in quest of minds that suppose that seeking someone out and making his acquaintance, indeed paying a simple visit, is degrading unless the nobility is involved. And if Socrates were to be reborn, a lofty gentleman would be ashamed

---

[84] In a letter to Lipsius, Marie de Gournay had already given a version of this passage: "C'est le bréviaire des demi-dieux, le contre-poison d'erreur, le hors de page des âmes, la résurrection de la verité, l'hellébore du sens humain et l'esprit de la raison" [It is the breviary of demi-gods, the antidote of error, the unwritten language of the soul, the resurrection of truth, the hellebore of human sense and the spirit of reason] ("Lettre du 25 avril 1593," Dezon-Jones, ed., *Discours féminin*, 188).

estat de le visiter seullement; ou, si la curiosité luy donnoit quelque envie de l'aborder, il s'en contenteroit pour une fois comme du spectacle des tableaux, affin de s'en retourner chez luy bien satisfaict, à son advis, au desir qu'il avoit eu de veoir un hault entendement, quand il en auroit contemplé la boette entre deux yeux. On veoit le ciel mesme en un moment, mais il faut du temps à veoir un esprit, autant qu'à l'instruire. Qui n'accointe que la qualité, c'est signe qu'il n'a que la qualité. S'il estoit plus galland homme qu'il n'est monsieur, il chercheroit un galland homme avant un monsieur. Mais c'estoit aux Roys Attales et Ptolomées à donner aux premieres ames les premieres places en leurs palais et en leur societé[68]; car ils avoient trop de suffisance pour pouvoir estre entretenuz, à leur poinct, d'autres que des plus habilles cervelles; et si avoient tant de merites qu'ils eussent trop plus perdu que leurs compaignons à n'acquerir pour amys ceux qui les sçauroient produire sur le Theatre de la posterité. Cependant si ceste humeur de ne se prendre qu'aux conditions et de mespriser les hommes dont les grades sont au dessoubz de soy, ne tombe, non point en un Monarque, mais au plus eslevé des Monarques, je ne vois pas qu'outre son ineptie elle ne soit encore plus injurieuse à son hoste qu'à autruy, le rendant apparié de dix millions de viles, sottes et vicieuses testes, qui seront au monde de mesme rang que luy, pour huppé qu'il soit, et justement desdaignable à tel et si grand nombre d'autres qu'il en est qui le surpassent en cela. N'a-il point de honte de ne s'estimer que par un poinct auquel, selon son ordonnance mesme, tant de millions de personnes le doibvent mespriser? et encore quel homme d'honneur n'auroit desdain de recevoir pour son amy celuy qui confesse que tant de gens se feroient honte de l'accepter à tel?

Or, retournant à mon propos, les grands esprits sont desireux, amoureux, et affolez des grands esprits: comme tenans leur estre du

---

[68] «Roys Attales et Ptolemées»: allusion aux rois de Pergame et d'Egypte, plusieurs fois évoqués dans les *Essais* (II, 2, 341 C; I 46, 276 A; etc.).

to report merely having called on him; or, if curiosity produced some desire to encounter him, the gentleman would be content to do so on a single occasion, as with a viewing of pictures, so that he might turn round and go home well satisfied, in his own opinion, with respect to his desire to see a high intelligence, when what he would have contemplated was the box it came in, located between two eyes. One sees even the heavens in an instant, but it takes time to see an intellect, as much as to form one. When someone consorts only with the nobly born, it is a sign that noble birth is all he has. If he were more a man of distinguished thought and feeling[85] than a lord, he would seek out such a man before a lord. But it was the part of the kings Attalus and Ptolemy[86] to assign to the foremost souls the foremost places in their palaces and their societies; for their sufficiency was too great to allow them to be conversed with, to their full measure, by other than the most able minds; and indeed they had such merits that they would have lost too much more than would their companions in not acquiring as friends those who could bring them forth in the Theater of Posterity.[87] Nevertheless, if that humor of being interested only in social rank and disdaining men of lower station gives way, not just in a monarch but in the most exalted of monarchs, I do not see why, unless he is stupid, it should not be yet more injurious to its possessor than to others, matching him with ten million vile, foolish, and vicious minds, which will be on the same level in the world as himself, however highly placed he may be, and making him justly contemptible to such others as there are—and there are a great number—who surpass him in this respect. Is it not shameful to value himself only for a quality in which, according to his own prescription, so many millions of persons must look down on him? And then, what man of honor would not disdain to receive as his friend one who confesses that so many people would be ashamed to accept him as such?

    Now, to return to my point, great minds desire, love, are mad for great minds, as if deriving their being from movement, and their prime

---

[85] The French is "galland homme," whose meaning is highly dependent on the cultural context.

[86] The kings, respectively, of Pergamum and Egypt, referred to many times in the *Essais* (Villey, ed., 2.2.341[C] [trans. Florio, 2: 17]; 1.46.276[A] [trans. Florio, 1: 312]; etc.). Marie de Gournay's text reads "Attales" for "Attalus."

[87] Marie de Gournay here adapts a commonplace metaphor (cf. the Theater of Life, the Theater of the World, etc.).

mouvement, et leur prime mouvement de la rencontre d'un pareil. Desassemblez les rouës de l'horologe, elles cessent; r'alliez-les sans changer de matiere ny de forme, il semble qu'en cet alliage seul elles chargent quelque image de vie, par une agitation perpetuelle. C'est abus de faire le sage et le seul ensemble, si la fortune ne refuze un second. Il est vray qu'un amy n'est pas un second, ny l'amitié n'est plus joincture ny liaison; c'est une double vie: estre amy, c'est estre deux fois. Il n'est pas homme qui peult vivre seul; et est chetif, à qui moins qu'un grand homme peut oster la solitude. Estre seul, c'est n'estre que demy[69]. Mais combien est encore plus miserable celuy qui demeure demy soy-mesme, pour avoir perdu l'autre part, qu'à faulte de l'avoir rencontré! Il y a mille arguments pour impugner ceux qui disent qu'une belle ame peut vivre heureuse sans l'alliance d'une autre, à fin d'excuser leur stupidité qui les empesche de la chercher, à faulte de la pouvoir bien savourer; et qui le pourroit, ardroit apres la volupté de l'esprit qui naist principalement en ce commerce d'un semblable, estant la premiere de toutes les humaines, par consequence necessaire de la preéminence qu'il a sur chaqu'une des parties de l'homme. Ce n'est plus sa commodité ny son contentement qui la porte à ceste recherche; c'est la preignante necessité de sortir du desert: et n'est pas grande, si la foulle n'est desert pour elle. A qui voullez vous qu'elle donne cognoissance de soy, s'elle ne trouve sa pareille? ou, s'il importe peu de se faire cognoistre à qui ne le peut estre, qu'il ne soit preferé sur le demeurant des hommes, aymé, chery, voire adoré?

Quoy? si quelque Monarque estoit reduit parmy des peuples où parce que sa dignité seroit ignorée, il fust mis entre les chartiers, ne souhaiteroit il point d'extreme ardeur de rencontrer quelqu'un qui recognoissant sa condition s'escriast: «C'est le Roy» et luy rendist son reng?

---

[69] Echos de l'essai «De l'Amitié»: «C'est un assez grand miracle de se doubler. [...] Nous estions à moitié de tout. [...] Il me semble n'estre plus qu'à demy» (I, 28, 191 A, 193 A).

movement from meeting one like them. Take apart the wheels of the clock: they stop; put them back together without changing either matter or form, and it seems that in this very fitting together they assume a certain image of life by a perpetual activity. It is wrong to play the sage and the solitary man at the same time, if fortune does not deny a second. Truly, a friend is not a second person, and friendship is not a joining or binding; it is a double life: to be a friend is to be twice. There is no man who can live alone; and he is a feeble one whose solitude can be relieved by less than a great man. To be alone is only to half-exist.[88] But how much more miserable is he who remains half himself for having lost his other part than one who is so for having failed to meet him! There are a thousand arguments to impugn those who say that one rare spirit can live happy without the alliance of another in order to excuse their stupidity, which keeps them from seeking one out instead of being able to enjoy one; and whoever is so able would burn for the mental pleasure that is born principally in this interchange with a soul-mate, since it is the foremost of all human pleasures, as necessarily follows from the preeminence that the mind has above all the parts of a human being. It is neither its comfort nor its satisfaction that draws the soul to this search; it is the pressing need to get out of the desert; and the soul is not great if the masses do not comprise a desert for it. To whom would you wish this spirit to make itself known, if it does not find its equal? Or, if there is little point in making itself known to one who cannot be such, is that person not to be preferred above the rest of mankind, beloved, cherished, indeed adored?

After all, if some monarch were reduced to the level of the common people, where, his greatness being unknown, he were placed with the cart-drivers, would he not wish with extreme longing to encounter someone who, recognizing his condition, would cry, "It is the King," and render him his rank?[89] Who indeed could cause beauty to

---

[88] Echoes of the essay "De l'amitié [Of Friendship]": "C'est un assez grand miracle de se doubler.... Nous estions à moitié de tout.... il me semble n'estre plus qu'à demy [It is a great and strange wonder for a man to double himselfe.... We were co-partners in all things.... me thinks I am but halfe my selfe]" (Villey, ed., 1.28.191[A] and 193[A]; trans. Florio, 1: 205 and 207).

[89] An apparent reminiscence, and displacement to the monarch's perspective, of Montaigne's account (in "De l'incommodité de la grandeur [Of the Incommoditie of Greatnesse]") of two competing views of greatness: "le populaire rend le Roy de pire condition qu'un charretier [The popular makes the King to be of worse condition then a Carter]" (Villey, ed., 3.7.918[B]; trans. Florio, 3: 154).

Qui pourroit seullement faire patienter à la beauté de vivre entre des aveugles? ou à la delicate voix de Neron de ne chanter qu'aux sourdz[70]? Estre incognu c'est aucunement n'estre pas; car estre se refere à l'agir; et n'est point, ce semble, d'agir parfaict, vers qui n'est pas capable de le gouster. Si ce poinct, au reste, est ambition, aumoins ne sommes nous pas assez honteux pour la desadvouer; c'est qu'un sage languit s'il ne peult rendre un homme de bien tesmoing de la pureté de sa conscience, au prix de ceste tourbe vulgaire; de son desengagement des erreurs communes et privées dont elle affole, combien il approche de Dieu plus pres qu'elle, combien il pourroit faire de mal qu'il ne veult pas, combien il feroit meilleur se fier et commettre à luy qu'au reste du monde, et de quelle sorte il sçauroit bien-heurer son amy par sa vie ou le rachepter par sa mort. A qui veut-on apres qu'il declare tant de belles conceptions? qu'il confere et discoure (seul plaisir qui peut, sinon esbatre, au moings arrester et fonder une ame forte) sinon à quelque suffisance semblable? Celuy qu'on relegue seul aux profondz desertz d'Arabie n'a rien de pis que cela, de ne veoir qui le ressemble, le congnoisse ny l'entende. A qui communiquera il tant de choses qu'il ne sçauroit taire sans se gehenner, ny les dire sans interest (par la tyrannie de la coustume sur la raison, ou quelque autre inconvenient) si ce n'est à une oreille saine? Avecq qui se peut-il mocquer seurement de la sottize des hommes, tousjours tres forcenée et le plus souvent si ruyneuse à son maistre propre qu'il semble qu'il ait gagé et entrepris, comme à prix faict, de s'esgorger pour blesser autruy: ne louant jamais son voisin pour sage sinon quand, par son exemple, il luy deffend d'estre heureux? La cognoissance de cette chetifve condition humaine[71], ne luy permettant pas aussi de s'asseurer ny qu'il face ny qu'il juge bien sans l'approbation d'un grand tesmoing, l'oblige à desirer un surveillant. Où veult-on apres qu'il exploicte la vigueur de ses mœurs, la douceur de sa conversation, sa foy, sa constance, ses affections et ses offices? Ceux qui soustiennent icy le party contraire disent qu'ils les respandent sur le peuple pour contrefaire une beneficence plus generalle. Certes, c'est, au contraire, ou qu'ils n'en trouvent point chez eux, ou qu'ils les y trouvent si maigres qu'ils n'en font pas grand compte; car de ce qu'on donne à chascun, on n'en

---

[70] Néron croyait posséder une voix très mélodieuse. Montaigne le cite 17 fois dans les *Essais*.

[71] Cf. «l'humaine condition» chez Montaigne (III, 2, 805 B).

be patient, living amongst the blind, or the delicate voice of Nero to sing only to the deaf?[90] To be unknown is, in a way, not to be; for being has reference to acting, and action can hardly be brought to perfection, it seems, when directed towards someone who cannot relish it. If that point, moreover, is ambition, at least we are not so shameful as to disavow it; a wise man languishes if he cannot make someone honorable a witness to the purity of his conscience in contrast with that vulgar crowd—to his exemption from the errors, common and private, that they are mad for; to how much closer he comes to God than they do, how much evil he could do that he does not wish to, how much better he would do to entrust and commit himself to that person than to the rest of the world, and in what manner he might gratify his friend by his life or redeem him by his death. To whom does one wish him, next, to declare so many beautiful conceptions, with whom to confer and discourse (the only pleasure that can, if not amuse, at least fix and ground a strong soul), unless with someone of like sufficiency? He whom one exiles alone to the deepest deserts of Arabia endures nothing worse than this—to see no one who would resemble him, know him, or listen to him. To whom will he communicate so many things that he could not keep to himself without suffering nor tell without detriment (because of the tyranny of custom over reason or some other liability), if not to a sound ear? With whom can he safely mock the folly of mankind, mad as it always is and most often so ruinous to its own possessor that it appears he has engaged and undertaken, as if at an agreed price, to cut his own throat to harm someone else, never praising his neighbor as wise except when, by his example, he forbids him to be happy? Knowledge of this feeble human condition,[91] by not permitting him to be so assured as to do or judge well without the approval of a substantial witness, compels him to desire an onlooker. Then, where does one wish him to employ the vigor of his way of life, the sweetness of his conversation, his faith, his constancy, his affections, and his duties? Those who maintain the contrary position on this say that they pour these out upon the people so as to produce by imitation a more general benefit. Surely, on the contrary, either they do not find them there at all or they find them in such meager form that they scarcely notice; for from what

---

[90] Nero believed himself possessed of a highly melodious voice. Montaigne mentions him seventeen times in the *Essais*.

[91] Cf. "l'humaine condition [humane condition]" in Montaigne (Villey, ed., 3.2.805[B]; trans. Florio, 3: 23–24).

tient personne et personne ne s'en tient plus riche. Et puis, il n'y a nulle apparence que ce present là, dont ils estiment un crocheteur digne, ils l'estimassent apres digne de Platon. Il fault bien prester au vulgaire sa vertu, mais il ne la fault donner qu'à la vertu mesme. Et n'est pas vertu bien à poinct s'il la peult toute employer; et si ne luy sçauroit rester des parties vacantes sans laesion; je dis laesion en son propre estre, d'autant qu'elle est action. Imaginez où vous reduirez Milo si vous luy deffendez la luitte et luy liez les bras[72].

Au surplus, qui mesurera le desir et la commodité qu'un sage a d'un autre sage, mesurera le desgoust et l'incommodité qu'il est à un sot. Il s'appelle la touche où s'espreuve le bon et le faux or; car selon l'estat et recherche que chascun en faict, il declare quel il est. La vigueur de ceste teste qui sert de delices à l'habile, c'est justement ce qui foule et froisse l'ignare[73]; et la clairvoiance estrangere n'est pas plus opportune à qui vault beaucoup qu'elle est importune à qui vault peu. Si vous cognoissez cettuy-cy, vous le ruinez; il n'a bien que d'estre pris pour un autre. C'est pourquoy, quand on m'a rapporté qu'il y eust quelque estroicte intelligence entre deux personnes, si tost que j'en ay cognu l'une, je me suis

---

[72] Milon de Crotone. Cf. *supra*, note 38.
[73] Echo de l'«Apologie de Raymond Sebon»: «Le moyen que je prens pour rabatre cette frenaisie [...] c'est de *froisser* et *fouler* aux pieds l'orgueil et humaine fierté» (II, 12, 448 A).

one gives to each, one gains a hold on nobody, and nobody comes out the richer for it. What is more, there is no indication that this gift, of which they esteem a porter worthy, they would afterwards esteem worthy of Plato.[92] One must indeed lend one's virtue to the vulgar, but one must not give it except to virtue itself. And it is by no means well regulated virtue if a person can employ all of it, and if there cannot remain to him, without detriment, some unused parts; I say detriment to his own being, insofar as it is action. Imagine to what you will reduce Milon if you forbid him to wrestle and bind his arms.[93]

What is more, whoever will measure the desire and pleasure that one wise man experiences with respect to another will measure the distaste and annoyance that belong to a fool. The sage is the real touchstone by which true and false gold are tested; for each man declares which he is by his attitude towards and search for such a one. The strength of that mind in which the able man delights is precisely what tramples and crumples the ignoramus,[94] and discernment on the part of another is no less welcome to someone of great value than it is unwelcome to someone of small account. If you know this man, you ruin him; his only resource is to be taken for another. This is why, when I have been told that there was some intimate understanding between two persons, as soon as I was acquainted with one of them, I was confident

---

[92] Marie de Gournay's mention of the "porter" ("crocheteur") confirms the inverse relation with "De l'incommodité de la grandeur [Of the Incommoditie of Greatnesse]," where Montaigne (following Plutarch [Villey, ed., 1321, n. to 918, line 35]) points out that, by contrast with deferential human beings, "un cheval, qui n'est ny flateur ny courtisan, verse le fils du Roy à terre comme il feroit le fils d'un crocheteur [*a horse who is neyther a flatterer nor a Courtier, will as soone throw the child of a King as the son of a base porter*]" (Villey, ed., 3.7.918[B]; trans. Florio, 3: 154). While her emphasis is on intellectual rather than merely social superiority, Marie de Gournay tends to see things the other way round. Cf. her insistence that "the soul is not great if the masses do not comprise a desert for it" (above, 89) with Montaigne's scorn for those who defer to princes in "les essays que nous faisons les uns contre les autres, par jalousie d'honneur et de valeur, soit aux exercices du corps, ou de l'esprit, ausquels la grandeur souveraine n'a aucune vraye part [the *Essayes*, which we through jealousie of honour or valour, make one against another, be it in the exercise of the body or minde: wherein soveraigne greatnesse, hath no true or essentiall part]" (Villey, ed., 3.7.918 B; trans. Florio, 3: 154).
[93] Milon of Croton; see above, n. 49.
[94] "[C]e qui foule et froisse l'ignare." An echo of the "Apologie de Raimond Sebond [An Apologie of *Raymond Sebond*]": "Le moyen que je prens pour rabatre cette frenaisie ... c'est de froisser et fouler aux pieds l'orgueil et humaine fierté [The meanes I use to suppress this frenzy ... is to crush, and trample this humane pride and fiercenesse under foot]" (Villey, ed., 2.12.448[A]; trans. Florio, 2: 137).

asseurée de les cognoistre toutes deux. *Pares cum paribus*, disent les clercs⁷⁴. Vous ne pouvez apparier à mesme timon un foible et un fort cheval: tous deux s'empescheroient et se harasseroient esgallement. Et qui voudra multiplier cet exemple jusques à l'amour: qu'un galland homme eschappast à Theano⁷⁵ et qu'un lourdault s'y prist sont choses, à mon advis, autant impossibles l'une que l'autre. La peau d'un sot est trop dure pour se coupper d'un couteau si delicat. Vous ne sçauriez attraper un bufle avec un las de soye: si feriez bien un Phoenix.

En fin, suyvant nostre fil, je croy que mon Pere eust esté d'opinion que quiconque prefereroit la sagesse de Socrates mesme au parfaict amy⁷⁶, si Dieu l'en mettoit au choix, ne sçauroit ny pourquoy celle là se donne, ny combien cettuy-cy vault; ou bien il se sentiroit incapable de sa fruition; et, de vray, quiconque est capable d'aymer et d'estre aymé comme nous l'entendons n'est incapable de rien. Le miserable qui le pert, il survit une perte racheptable de la sagesse de Socrates. Qui l'a eu et perdu n'a plus qu'esperer ny craindre; car il a preoccupé le Paradis et l'Enfer⁷⁷. Et Pythias survivant à Damon, vous dira que, s'il n'a perdu

---

⁷⁴ «Qui se ressemble, s'assemble».

⁷⁵ Epouse ou bru de Pythagore, elle était d'une sagesse légendaire. Cf. *Egalité des Hommes et des Femmes,* éd. Dezon-Jones, p. 115. Dans l'éloge qu'il fit de Marie de Gournay, Juste Lipse prédisait que celle-ci deviendrait la véritable Théano de son époque. Cf. *Epistolarum Centuria Secunda* (1590) cité dans Dezon-Jones, p. 25. Voir aussi *Essais,* I, 21, 101 C.

⁷⁶ Ceci rappelle le parallèle montaignien entre Socrate et le «parfaict amy», posé dans l'essai «De la Phisionomie» (III, 12, 1057 B et C).

⁷⁷ Nouveaux échos, ici et dans les lignes suivantes, de l'essai «De l'Amitié»: «Depuis le jour que je le perdy, [...] je ne fay que trainer languissant; et les plaisirs mesmes qui s'offrent à moy, au lieu de me consoler, me redoublent le regret de sa perte» (I, 28, 193 A).

of knowing them both. *Pares cum paribus*, say the learned.⁹⁵ You cannot couple to the same wagon-tongue a weak horse and a strong one: each would equally hinder and hamper the other. And if one wishes to multiply that instance as far as love, that a man of distinguished thought and feeling should escape the charms of Theano⁹⁶ and that a lout should succumb to them are, in my view, impossible things, each as much as the other. The skin of a fool is too tough to be cut by such a fine knife. You cannot catch a buffalo with a silken net, but you would do well with a phoenix.

Finally, to follow our thread, I believe that my Father would have been of the opinion that whoever should prefer the wisdom of Socrates himself to the perfect friend,⁹⁷ if God put him to the choice, would not know either why that wisdom was bestowed or how much that friend was worth; or, rather, he would sense himself incapable of its fruition; and, truly, whoever is capable of loving and being loved, as we understand it, is incapable of nothing. The miserable person who loses such a friend survives a loss that it would take the wisdom of Socrates to redeem. Whoever has possessed and lost him has nothing more to hope or to fear; for he has already occupied Paradise and hell.⁹⁸ And Pythias, surviving Damon, will tell you that, if he has not lost himself,

---

⁹⁵ "Like will to like." Under this heading, *The Oxford Dictionary of English Proverbs* (comp. William George Smith, 3rd ed., rev. F. P. Wilson [Oxford: Clarendon Press, 1970]), 465, cites Cicero, *De Senectute* 3.7: "Pares autem vetere proverbio cum paribus facillime congregantur" [Equals, moreover, most readily gather with equals, according to the old proverb].

⁹⁶ The spouse or daughter-in-law of Pythagoras, she was of a legendary wisdom. Cf. *Égalité des hommes et des femmes*, ed. Dezon-Jones, *Discours féminin*, 115. In a letter of praise to Marie de Gournay, Lipsius predicted that she would become the veritable Theano of her age (Dezon-Jones, ed., 25). See also the *Essais*, Villey, ed., 1.21.101(C); trans. Florio, 1: 97.

⁹⁷ Montaigne actually parallels Socrates and his own "perfect friend" La Boétie in the essay "De la phisionomie [Of Phisiognomy]" (Villey, ed., 3.12.1057[B,C]; trans. Florio, 3: 314).

⁹⁸ There are new echoes, here and in the following lines, of the essay "De l'amitié [Of Friendship]": "Depuis le jour que je le perdy, ... je ne fay que trainer languissant; et les plaisirs mesmes qui s'offrent à moy, au lieu de me consoler, me redoublent le regret de sa perte [Since the time I lost him, ... I doe but languish, I doe but sorrow: and even those pleasures, all things present me with, in stead of yeelding me comfort, doe but redouble the griefe of his losse]" (Villey, ed., 1.28.193[A]; trans. Florio, 1: 207).

soy-mesme, aumoins a-il perdu la moitié qui le mettoit en possession de l'autre[78]. Sa condition n'est plus vivre, c'est souffrir; car il n'est plus que par son mal-heur. Il n'est plus en effect; ou, s'il est, c'est comme un paralytique qui survit à la meilleure part de ses membres propres; car son estre estoit non pas joinct, mais infuz à celuy de son amy. Sa volonté mesme, sa liberté, sa raison luy restent desormais comme excremens inutiles, d'autant qu'il s'estoit accoustumé de ne les sçavoir plus jouyr que par les mains d'un autre. Et si avoit appris, en ce cher usage, qu'on ne les peut heureusement posseder qu'en la douce et fidelle garde d'un amy. Certes, il n'est plus du tout; car s'il estoit plus amy qu'il n'estoit homme ny soy-mesme, ains s'il s'estoit transformé d'homme et de soy-mesme en amy, n'estant plus amy comment seroit il? Sa conservation n'est autre chose que celle de ceste chere teste; car il s'est perdu en soy, pour se recouvrer en autruy[79]. Estre amy c'est n'estre que depositaire de soy-mesme. La plus grande infelicité du monde c'est d'avoir la plus grande felicité; je l'avois en ce tres-grand Pere, puis qu'il en fault achepter la possession terminée au prix de la privation perpetuelle.

Mon ame a refusé cent fois obeyssance à ce mien dessein d'escrire un mot sur les *Essays,* me representant l'impuissance qui luy reste parmy le trouble où ma calamité la precipite, et que ce n'est icy le lieu de parler de la tres-saincte et tres-chere societé d'où la mort m'arrache, ny sa faculté, d'elle, de s'entretenir d'autre chose. Lecteur, n'accuse pas de temerité le favorable jugement qu'il a faict de moy, quand tu

---

[78] Damon et Pythias, philosophes pythagoriciens, célèbres pour leur amitié exemplaire. Dans l'Epître dédicatoire du *Proumenoir,* Marie de Gournay fait allusion à «la dilection tres-saincte de Pithias et de Damon [qui] fut inviolable» (p. 2).

[79] On retrouve les mêmes termes chez Montaigne, la volonté de l'un allant «se plonger et se perdre» dans celle de l'autre. «Je dis *perdre,* à la vérité, ne nous reservants rien qui nous fut propre, ny qui fut sien ou mien» (I, 28, 189 A et C).

at least he has lost the half that he put in possession of the other.[99] His condition is no longer living—it is suffering; for he no longer exists, except through his misery. Indeed, he no longer is; or, if he is, it is like a paralytic who lives on after the best part of his own limbs; for his being was not joined to but infused in that of his friend. His very will, his liberty, his reason remain henceforth like useless appendages, inasmuch as he had accustomed himself not to know how to use them any more except by the hands of another. And so he had learned, in that precious employment of them, that one cannot possess them happily except in the sweet and faithful keeping of a friend. Indeed, he no longer is at all; for really he was more a friend than he was a person or himself, and, if he were transformed from a person and from himself into a friend, no longer being a friend, how could he be? Preserving himself means nothing but preserving that precious life; for he has lost himself in himself to recover himself in another.[100] To be a friend is to exist only as the depositary of oneself. The greatest unhappiness in the world is to have the greatest happiness; I had this in that greatest of Fathers, since I must pay for my expired possession of him with perpetual deprivation.

My soul has a hundred times refused to comply with this intention of mine to write a word about the *Essays*, representing to me the feebleness it still possesses amidst the trouble into which my calamity has plunged it, and that here is not the place to speak of the most sacred and precious companionship from which death has torn me, nor does it have the capacity to converse on other subjects. Reader, do not accuse of rashness the favorable judgment that he made of me, when

---

[99] Damon and Pythias, Pythagorean philosophers celebrated for their exemplary friendship. In the dedicatory "Epistre" [Epistle] to *Le Proumenoir*, Marie de Gournay affirms that while natural relations, even between fathers and children, have often proved lacking in affection, "la dilection tressaincte de Pithias & de Damon . . . fut inviolable" [the most holy devotion of Pythias and Damon . . . was inviolable] (*Le Proumenoir de Monsieur de Montaigne [1594]: A Facsimile Reproduction with an Introduction by Patricia Francis Cholakian*, ed. Patricia Francis Cholakian [Delmar, NY: Scholars' Facsimiles and Reprints, 1985], fol. 3ʳ).

[100] One finds the same terms in Montaigne, the will of one going forth "se plonger et se perdre [to plunge and lose it selfe]" in that of the other: "Je dis perdre, à la verité, ne nous reservant rien qui nous fut propre, ny qui fut sien ou mien [I may truly say, lose, reserving nothing unto us, that might properly be called our owne, nor that was either his, or mine]" (Villey, ed., 1.28.189[A]; trans. Florio, 1: 202). Marie de Gournay's language conforms to that commonly associated with the Neoplatonic ideas then widespread in France.

considereras, en cet escrit icy, combien je suis loing de le meriter⁸⁰. Lors qu'il me loüoit, je le possedois; moy avec luy, et moy sans luy, sommes absoluement deux. Il ne m'a duré que quatre ans, non plus qu'à luy La Boetie⁸¹. Seroit ce que la fortune par pitié des autres hommes eust limité telles amitiez à ce terme, affin que le mespris d'une fruition si courte les gardast de s'engager aux douleurs qu'il fault souffrir de la privation? Gueres de gens ne seront dangereux pourtant de broncher à ce pas; chacun a beau se mocquer seurement de nostre impatience et nous deffier en constance; car nul ne peut perdre autant que nous. Ils demandent où est la raison: la raison mesme c'est aymer en ces amitiez. On ne plaint pas ce mal-heur qui veut; car voicy le seul mot du contract au marché de l'amitié perfaicte: Toy et moy nous rendons l'un à l'autre, par ce que nous ne sçaurions si bien rencontrer ailleurs⁸². Il est mort à cinquante neuf ans l'an 1592 d'une fin si fameuse en tous les poinctz de sa perfection qu'il n'est pas besoin que je le publie d'avantage⁸³. Bien en publieray-je, si l'entendement me dure, les circonstances particulieres alors que je les sçauray fort exactement par la bouche de ceux mesmes qui les ont recueillies (car plusieurs autres tesmoings n'ont sçeu confirmer ma creance) et recueillies avec le tendre à-Dieu qu'il commanda m'estre envoyé de sa part, de la main du sieur de la Brousse, son bon frere⁸⁴. Et le sieur de Bussaguet son cousin, qui

---

⁸⁰ Voir l'éloge de Marie de Gournay dans les *Essais* (II, 17, 661–662 C), éloge qui, d'ailleurs, apparaît pour la première fois dans l'édition de 1595, ce qui a fait supposer à certains qu'il était une addition de la «fille d'alliance».

⁸¹ Effectivement la rencontre avec La Boétie se situe en 1558–1559 et l'amitié qu'elle avait suscitée devait être interrompue par la mort de l'ami en août 1563. Marie de Gournay, elle, avait rencontré Montaigne à Paris en 1588, et celui-ci devait mourir quatre ans plus tard, le 13 septembre 1592.

⁸² Reformulation approximative du fameux *allongeail*: «par ce que c'estoit luy, parce ce que c'estoit moy» (I, 28, 188 C).

⁸³ Nous avons le témoignage d'Etienne Pasquier sur cette mort exemplaire: «Il fit dire la Messe dans sa chambre, et, comme le Prestre estoit sur l'eslevation du *Corpus Domini*, ce pauvre Gentilhomme s'eslance au moins mal qu'il peut, comme à corps perdu, sur son lit, les mains joinctes, et en ce dernier acte rendit son esprit à Dieu.» *Les Lettres d'Etienne Pasquier*, Paris, 1619, tome II, p. 377.

⁸⁴ Le sieur de la Brousse: frère de Montaigne, évoqué au début de l'essai «De la Conscience» (II, 5, 366 A). Marie de Gournay lui dédie un quatrain à la fin du *Proumenoir* (pp. 77–78).

you consider, in what is written here, how far I am from deserving it.[101] When he praised me, I possessed him; myself with him and myself without him are two different things. He was mine for only four years, no longer than La Boétie was his.[102] Might it be that fortune, out of pity for other human beings, has limited such friendships to such a term, so that contempt for such a short period of enjoyment would keep them from falling into the torment that privation must engender? Yet scarcely anybody will be at risk of stumbling at that step; in vain, surely, all mock our lack of patience and challenge us in constancy; for no one can lose as much as we. They ask where reason is: it is reason itself to love in these friendships. Not just anyone commiserates with that unhappiness; for here are the only terms of the bargain for perfect friendship: you and I, we give ourselves to one another, because we cannot make so good a meeting elsewhere.[103] He died at the age of fifty-nine in the year 1592 with an end so well known in all its points of perfection that there is no need for me to publish it further.[104] Still, I will publish, if my mind holds out, the private circumstances belonging to it, when I know them with perfect exactitude from the mouths of those who collected them (for several other witnesses have not been in a position to confirm my opinion)—and collected them with the tender adieu that he commanded should be conveyed to me from him by the hand of Lord La Brousse, his good brother.[105] And Lord Bussaguet,

---

[101] See the tribute to Marie de Gournay in the *Essais* (Villey, ed., 2.17.661–662[C]; trans. Florio, 2: 389), a tribute that, moreover, appears for the first time in the edition of 1595; this fact has caused some to suppose it an addition made by the "adoptive daughter."

[102] Indeed, his meeting with La Boétie took place in 1558–1559, and the friendship to which it led was broken off by the death of his friend in August 1563. For her part, Marie de Gournay had met Montaigne in Paris in 1588, and he died four years later on 13 September 1592.

[103] Approximate reformulation of the famous addition: "Par ce que c'estoit luy; parce ce que c'estoit moy [Because it was he, because it was my selfe]" (Villey, ed., 1.28.188[C]; trans. Florio, 1: 201).

[104] We have the testimony of Étienne Pasquier on that exemplary death: "Il fit dire la Messe dans sa chambre, et, comme le Prestre estoit sur l'eslevation du *Corpus Domini*, ce pauvre Gentilhomme s'eslance au moins mal qu'il peut, comme à corps perdu, sur son lit, les mains joinctes, et en ce dernier acte rendit son esprit à Dieu." [He had the mass said in his room and, as the priest arrived at the elevation of the host, that poor Gentleman threw himself as well as he could, as if his body were lost, upon his bed, his hands joined together, and in that final act rendered his spirit to God.] (*Les lettres d'Estienne Pasquier, etc.*, 3 vols. [Paris: L. Sonnius, 1619], 2: 377).

[105] Lord La Brousse: brother of Montaigne, referred to at the beginning of the essay "De la conscience [Of Conscience]" (Villey, ed., 2.5.366[A]; trans. Florio, 2: 44). Marie de Gournay dedicates a quatrain to him at the end of *Le Proumenoir* (77–78).

porte dignement le nom de la maison de Montaigne, à laquelle il sert d'un bon pillier depuis qu'elle a perdu le sien, ne me peut esclaircir de cela, quand je l'allay veoir exprez pour m'en instruire, à Chartres, où ses affaires le porterent il y a quelque annee, d'autant qu'il n'estoit pas present au decez[85].

Au surplus, la conduitte et succez de ce livre, conferé à la miserable incorrection qu'ont encouru les autres qui n'ont pas esté mis sur la presse du vivant de leur autheur, tesmoing ceux la de Turnebus[86], apprendra combien quelque bon Ange a monstré qu'il l'estimoit digne de particuliere faveur, veu mesme que non pas seulement la vigilance des Imprimeurs, à laquelle on les remet communement en telles occurrences, mais encore le plus esveillé soing que les amys ayent accoustumé d'y rendre, n'y pouvoit suffire. Parce qu'outre la naturelle difficulté de correction qui se void aux *Essays*, ceste copie en avoit tant d'autres que ce n'estoit pas legere entreprise que la bien lire, et garder que telle difficulté n'apportast ou quelque entente fauce, ou transposition, ou des obmissions.

Somme, apres que j'ay dict qu'il luy falloit un bon tuteur, j'ose me vanter qu'il ne luy en falloit, pour son bien, nul autre que moy, mon affection supplant à mon incapacité. Que je sçay de gré au sieur de Brach[87], de ce qu'il assista tousjours soigneusement madame de Montaigne[88] au premier soucy de sa fortune, intermettant pour cet exercice la Poesie dont il honnore sa Gascongne, et ne se contentant pas d'emporter sur le siecle present et les passez le tiltre d'unicque mary, par la gloire qu'il preste au nom de sa femme deffuncte, s'il n'envioit encore celuy de bon amy par tels offices, et plus meritoires vers un mort. Au reste, j'ay secondé ses inventions jusques à l'extreme superstition. Aussi n'eussé-je pas restivé, lors que j'eusse jugé quelque chose corrigeable, de

---

[85] Le sieur de Bussaguet: le plus jeune des quatre oncles de Montaigne. Son attitude favorable à la médecine lui porta malheur (II, 37, 765 B). Marie de Gournay lui dédie un quatrain à la fin du *Proumenoir* (p. 77).

[86] Turnebus: Adrien de Turnèbe, humaniste français (1512-1565). «Adrianus Turnebus sçavoit plus et sçavoit mieux ce qu'il sçavoit que homme qui fut de son siècle» (II, 17, 661 A). Cf. aussi I, 25, 139 A et II, 12, 440 A.

[87] Pierre de Brach (1548?-1605?), poète bordelais. Il aida la veuve de Montaigne à relever les additions et corrections portées sur l'exemplaire dit «de Bordeaux» et à en envoyer copie à Marie de Gournay. Celle-ci publia une «Ode au Sieur de Brach, sur le tombeau d'Aymée, sa femme» dans le *Proumenoir* (pp. 64-66).

[88] Madame de Montaigne: cf. *supra*, note 14.

his cousin, who worthily bears the name of the house of Montaigne, to which he has served as a strong pillar since it lost its own, could not enlighten me on that point when, expressly to be informed about it, I went to see him at Chartres (where his business took him about a year ago), inasmuch as he was not present at the death.[106]

What is more, the course and success of that book, which was consigned to the wretched state of incorrectness encountered by others not put through the press while their authors were living—witness those of Turnebus[107]—will indicate to what extent some good angel has made known that he esteemed it worthy of particular favor, in view of the fact that not only the vigilance of the printers, to which one commonly entrusts books in such situations, but even the most alert care that friends have been accustomed to give it could not have been sufficient for it. For, in addition to the natural difficulty of correction that presents itself in the *Essays*, that copy had so many others that it was no slight enterprise even to read it and to ensure that such difficulty did not introduce either some false meaning or transposition or omissions.

In sum, having said that it needed a worthy guardian, I dare to boast that it needed, for its own good, none other than myself, my affection making up for my incapacity. What thanks I owe Lord Brach[108] for having always attentively assisted Madame de Montaigne in the first cares of her fortune, interrupting, for the sake of that exercise, the poetry with which he honors his Gascony! And, not contenting himself with carrying away, above the ages present and past, the title of an unparalleled husband for the glory he lends to the name of his deceased wife, if he did not still desire to possess that of a good friend by such offices, all the more meritorious because for the sake of someone dead! Moreover, I have supported his arguments down to the last scruple. Nor

---

[106] Lord Bussaguet: the youngest of the four uncles of Montaigne. His favorable attitude to medical science caused trouble for him (Villey, ed., 2.37.765[B]; trans. Florio, 2: 498). He, too, has a quatrain dedicated to him at the end of *Le Proumenoir* (77).

[107] Turnebus: Adrien de Turnèbe, French Humanist (1512–1565). "Adrianus Turnebus sçavoit plus et sçavoit mieux ce qu'il sçavoit, que homme qui fut de son siecle, ny loing au delà [*Adrianus Turnebus* knew more and better, what he knew, than any man in his age or of many ages past]" (Villey, ed., 2.17.661[A]; trans. Florio, 2: 389). Cf. also Villey, ed., 1.25.139(A) (trans. Florio, 1: 142) and 2.12.440(A) (trans. Florio, 2: 128).

[108] Pierre de Brach (1548?–1605?), the poet from Bordeaux. He helped Montaigne's widow to collect the additions and corrections made to the so-called "Bordeaux edition" and to send a copy of them to Marie de Gournay. The latter published an "Ode au Sieur de Brach, sur le tombeau d'Aymée, sa femme" [Ode to Lord Brach on the Tomb of Aymée, His Wife] in *Le Proumenoir* (64–66).

plier et prosterner toutes les forces de mon discours, soubs ceste seulle consideration que celuy qui le voulut ainsin estoit Pere, et qu'il estoit Montaigne. Je le dis à fin d'empescher que ceux qui se rencontreront sur quelque phraze ou quelque obscurité, qui les arreste, pour s'amuser à drapper l'Impression comme s'elle avoit en cela trahy l'Autheur, ne perdent la queste du fruict, qui ne peut manquer d'y estre, puis qu'elle l'a plus qu'exactement suivy. Dont je pourrois appeler à tesmoing une autre copie qui reste en sa maison[89], n'estoit que je ne me defie pas que personne doubte de ma solicitude en ce qui luy touche. Ceux qui n'y peuvent penetrer, qu'ils ne s'en prennent qu'à eux mesmes; je n'y trouve passage non intelligible pour moy, qu'un; et quelque meilleur interprete m'apprendra peut estre à l'entendre.

Et en fin, jaçoit que ceste Impression, laquelle je fais achever en l'an mil cinq cens nonante et quatre, à Paris, ne soit pas parfaicte jusques à tel poinct que je desirois, si est-ce que je requiers qu'on s'addresse tousjours à elle: soit un Lecteur capable de juger combien les *Essays* meritent d'estre exactement cognus, soit tel qui les voudroit faire imprimer aux nations estrangeres. Par ce qu'outre cela qu'elle n'est pas si loing de la perfection qu'on soit asseuré si les suyvantes la pourront approcher d'aussi pres, elle est aumoins diligemment redressée par un *Errata*, sauf en quelques si legeres fautes qu'elles se restituent elles mesmes. Et de peur qu'on ne rejecte comme temerairement ingerez certains traictz de plume qui corrigent cinq ou six characteres ou que quelqu'un, à leur adveu, n'en meslast d'autres de sa teste, je donne advis qu'ils sont en ces mots: *si, demesler, deuils, osté, Indique, estacade, affreré, paelle, m'a, engagez*, et quelques poincts de moindre consequence. Je ne puis apporter trop de precaution ny de curiosité sur une chose de tel merite, et non mienne. Adieu Lecteur.

---

[89] L'édition de 1595 a donc été faite non pas d'après l'exemplaire de Bordeaux mais sur une transcription procurée à Marie de Gournay par la veuve de Montaigne à Paris. Cf. Richard A. Sayce and David Maskell, *A Descriptive Bibliography of Montaigne's «Essais», 1580–1700*, Londres, The Bibliographical Society et Oxford University Press, 1983, pp. 25–29.

would I have hesitated, when I had deemed something fit to be corrected, to bend and prostrate all the force of my reasoning beneath this sole consideration—that he who wished it thus was my Father, and that he was Montaigne. I say this in order to forestall that those who join in fixing on some phrase or obscurity, which stymies them, so as to amuse themselves by denigrating the printing, as if it betrayed the author in this respect, should lose out in the quest for the fruit, which cannot fail to be there, because the printing has followed him with more than exactitude. For which I could call to witness another copy that remains in his house,[109] were it not that I am not concerned that any person will doubt my solicitude in anything that relates to him. Those who cannot penetrate it, let them blame no one but themselves; I do not find there any passage not intelligible to myself, except one; and some better interpreter will perhaps teach me to understand it.

And finally, although this printing, which I have caused to be done in the year one thousand, five hundred and ninety-four, at Paris, is not perfect to the extent that I would wish, yet I ask that it always be referred to, whether one is a reader capable of judging how much the *Essays* deserve to be known in detail or the sort who would wish to have them printed abroad. For, besides the fact that it is not so far from perfection that one may be assured that those that follow could come as close as it does, it is at least diligently corrected by means of an *Errata*, except in some faults so minor that they rectify themselves. And out of fear lest certain strokes of the pen that correct five or six characters should be rejected as audaciously inserted, or that someone, on the basis of the admission that these make, should intermingle others out of his own head, I give notice that they are in the following words: *si, demesler, deuils, osté, Indique, estacade, affreré, paelle, m'a, engagez*, and certain points of less consequence. I cannot bring too much circumspection or careful examination to something of such merit—and not my own. Reader, adieu.

---

[109] The edition of 1595 was therefore prepared, not according to the Bordeaux copy, but on the basis of a transcription procured by Montaigne's widow for Marie de Gournay in Paris. Cf. Richard A. Sayce and David Maskell, *A Descriptive Bibliography of Montaigne's Essais, 1580–1700* (London: The Bibliographical Society and The Modern Humanities Research Association, 1983), 25–29.

Works Cited

Primary Sources

Dezon-Jones, Élyane, ed. *Fragments d'un discours féminin*. By Marie de Gournay. [Paris]: Corti, 1988.

Diogenes Laertius. *Lives of Eminent Philosophers*. Ed. and trans. R. D. Hicks. 2 vols. Loeb Classical Library. London: Heinemann; New York: Putnam's, 1925.

Erasmus, Desiderius. *Adages*. Trans. Margaret Mann Phillips. Annotated R. A. B. Mynors. Vols. 2–5 (vols. 3–5 trans. and annotated R. A. B. Mynors). *Collected Works of Erasmus*, vols. 31–34. Toronto: University of Toronto Press, 1982–1992.

Florio = Montaigne, Michel de. *Montaigne's Essays*. Trans. John Florio.

Gournay, Marie le Jars de. *Les Advis, ou, les Presens de la Demoiselle de Gournay 1641*. Gen. eds. Jean-Philippe Beaulieu and Hannah Fournier. 3 vols. Amsterdam and Atlanta, GA: Rodopi, 1997– .

———. *Égalité des hommes et des femmes, Grief des dames, Le Proumenoir de Monsieur de Montaigne*. Ed. Constant Venesoen. Textes Littéraires Français. Geneva: Droz, 1993.

———. *L'Ombre de la demoiselle de Gournay*. Paris: Jean Libert, 1626.

———. "Préface de 1599 publiée dans *Le Proumenoir*." Ed. Anna Lia Franchetti. *Montaigne Studies: An Interdisciplinary Forum* 8.1–2 (1996): 179–192.

———. "Préface to Montaigne's *Essais* (1595)." In *La première réception des* Essais *de Montaigne (1580–1640)*, ed. Olivier Millet, 79–128. Études montaignistes, 24. Paris: Champion, 1995.

———. "Preface to the 1617 Edition of the *Essais*." Ed. Mary McKinley. *Montaigne Studies: An Interdisciplinary Forum* 8.1–2 (1996): 203–219.

———. *Le Proumenoir de Monsieur de Montaigne*. Paris: Abel L'Angelier, 1594.

———. *Le Proumenoir de Monsieur de Montaigne (1594) by Marie le Jars de Gournay: A Facsimile Reproduction with an Introduction by Patricia Francis Cholakian*. Delmar, NY: Scholars' Facsimiles and Reprints, 1985.

Horace. *Horace, Odes and Epodes.* Trans. C. E. Bennett. Rev. ed. Loeb Classical Library. Cambridge, MA: Harvard University Press; London: Heinemann, 1927.

La Noue, François de. *Discours politiques et militaires, etc.* Basel: F. Forest, 1587.

Lipsius, Justus. *Justi Lipsii Epistolarum centuriae duae, etc.* 2 vols. in 1. Antwerp: C. Plantin, 1591.

Marguerite de Valois. *Mémoires et autres écrits de Marguerite de Valois, La Reine Margot.* Ed. Yves Cazaux. Paris: Mercure de France, 1986.

Montaigne, Michel de. *Les Essais de Michel de Montaigne: Édition conforme au texte de l'exemplaire de Bordeaux avec les additions de l'édition posthume, l'explication des termes vieillis et la traduction des citations, une étude sur Montaigne, une chronologie de sa vie et de son oeuvre, le catalogue de ses livres et la liste des inscriptions qu'il avait fait peindre dans sa librairie, des notices, des notes, un appendice sur l'influence des Essais, et un index.* Ed. Pierre Villey. New ed. with a Preface by V.-L. Saulnier. Paris: Presses Universitaires de France, 1965.

———. *Journal de voyage.* Ed. Fausta Garavini. Paris: Gallimard, 1983.

———. *Montaigne's Essays* (1603). Trans. John Florio. With an Introd. by L. C. Harmer. 3 vols. Everyman's Library. London: Dent; New York: Dutton, 1965.

Montluc, Blaise de. *Commentaires, etc.* Bordeaux: S. Millanges, 1592.

Nepos, Cornelius. *Cornelius Nepos.* Trans. John C. Rolfe. Loeb Classical Library. London: Heineman; New York: Putnam's, 1929.

Pascal, Blaise. *Pascal's Pensées.* Trans. and ed. H. F. Stewart. London: Routledge and Kegan Paul, 1950.

Pasquier, Étienne. *Les lettres d'Estienne Pasquier, etc.* 3 vols. Paris: L. Sonnius, 1619.

Pausanias. *Description of Greece.* Trans. W. H. S. Jones. 4 vols. Loeb Classical Library. Cambridge, MA: Harvard University Press; London: Heinemann, 1918-1935.

Petronius Arbiter. *Petronius.* Trans. Michael Heseltine. With Seneca, *Apocolocyntosis*, trans. W. H. D. Rouse. Loeb Classical Library. London: Heinemann; New York: Macmillan, 1913.

Plato. *Symposium.* Trans. Robin Waterfield. World's Classics. Oxford: Oxford University Press, 1994.

Pliny, the Elder. *Natural History.* Trans. H. Rackham. 10 vols. (vol. 7 ed. and trans. W. H. S. Jones). Loeb Classical Library. London: Heinemann; Cambridge, MA: Harvard University Press, 1938-1962.

Plutarch. *Plutarch's Lives.* Ed. and trans. Bernadotte Perrin. 11 vols. Loeb Classical Library. Cambridge, MA: Harvard University Press; London: Heinemann, 1914–1926.

La saincte Bible . . . Traduicte de Latin en François par les Théologiens de l'Université de Louvain, etc. 1572; Lyon: Thibaud Ancelin, 1603.

Uildriks, Anne, ed. *Les idées littéraires de Mlle de Gournay: Réédition de ses traités philologiques des* Advis et presens, *édition de 1641 avec les variantes des éditions de 1626 et de 1634; et réédition de sa préface des* Essais *de Montaigne, édition de 1635 avec les variantes de 1595 et de 1599.* Groningen: Kleine, [1962].

Villey, ed. = Montaigne, Michel de. *Essais.* Ed. Pierre Villey.

Secondary Sources

Abel, Günter. "Juste Lipse et Marie de Gournay autour de *l'exemplaire d'Anvers* des *Essais* de Montaigne." *Bibliothèque d'Humanisme et Renaissance* 35 (1973): 117–129.

Albistur, Maïté, and Daniel Armogathe. *Histoire du féminisme français du moyen âge à nos jours.* 2 vols. [Paris]: Éditions Des Femmes, 1977.

Allen, Don Cameron. *Doubt's Boundless Sea: Skepticism and Faith in the Renaissance.* Baltimore, MD: The Johns Hopkins Press, 1964.

Arnould, Jean-Claude, ed. *Marie de Gournay et l'édition de 1595 des* Essais *de Montaigne: Actes du Collogue organisé par la Société Internationale des Amis de Montaigne (9–10 juin 1995).* Paris: Champion, 1996.

Bauschatz, Cathleen M. "Imitation, Writing, and Self-Study in Marie de Gournay's 1595 'Préface' to Montaigne's *Essais.*" In *Contending Kingdoms: Historical, Psychological, and Feminist Approaches to the Literature of Sixteenth-Century England and France,* ed. Marie-Rose Logan and Peter L. Rudnytsky, 346–364. Detroit, MI: Wayne State University Press, 1991.

———. "Marie de Gournay's 'Préface de 1595': A Critical Evaluation." *Bulletin de la Société des Amis de Montaigne* 3-4 (1986): 73–82.

Boase, Alan M. *The Fortunes of Montaigne: A History of the* Essais *in France, 1580–1669.* 1935; repr. New York: Octagon, 1970.

Bonnefon, Paul. *Montaigne et ses amis: La Boétie, Charron, Mlle de Gournay.* 2 vols. 1898; repr. Geneva: Slatkine, 1969.

———. "Une supercherie de Mlle de Gournay." *Revue d'histoire littéraire de la France* 3 (1896): 71–89.

Cholakian, Patricia Francis. Introduction. In *Le Proumenoir de Monsieur*

de Montaigne (1594) by Marie le Jars de Gournay: A Facsimile Reproduction with an Introduction by Patricia Francis Cholakian*, 7–45. Delmar, NY: Scholars' Facsimiles and Reprints, 1985.

Desan, Philippe. "The Book, the Friend, the Woman: Montaigne's Circular Exchanges." Trans. Brad Bassler. In *Contending Kingdoms: Historical, Psychological, and Feminist Approaches to the Literature of Sixteenth-Century England and France*, ed. Marie-Rose Logan and Peter L. Rudnytsky, 225–262. Detroit, MI: Wayne State University Press, 1991.

Dezon-Jones, Élyane. Introduction. In *Fragments d'un discours féminin*, by Marie de Gournay, ed. Élyane Dezon-Jones, 9–108. [Paris]: Corti, 1988.

———. "Marie de Gournay: le je/u/ palimpseste." *L'Esprit créateur* 23.2 (1983): 26–36.

Donne, John. *The Complete Poetry of John Donne*. Ed. John T. Shawcross. Garden City, NY: Doubleday Anchor, 1967.

Franchetti, Anna Lia. "Marie de Gournay apologiste des *Essais*: la préface de 1599." *Montaigne Studies: An Interdisciplinary Forum* 8.1–2 (1996): 173–177.

Haydn, Hiram. *The Counter-Renaissance*. New York: Harcourt, 1950.

Hillman, Richard. "*Hamlet* et la Préface de Marie de Gournay." *Renaissance and Reformation/Renaissance et Réforme* n.s. 18 (1994): 29–42.

———. *Self-Speaking in Medieval and Early Modern English Drama: Subjectivity, Discourse and the Stage*. Basingstoke, Hampshire: Macmillan; New York: St. Martin's, 1997.

Holmes, Peggy P. "Mlle de Gournay's Defence of Baroque Imagery." *French Studies* 8 (1954): 122–131.

Horowitz, Maryanne Cline. "Marie de Gournay, Editor of the *Essais* of Michel de Montaigne: A Case-Study in Mentor-Protégée Friendship." *Sixteenth Century Journal* 17 (1986): 271–284.

Ilsley, Marjorie Henry. *A Daughter of the Renaissance: Marie le Jars de Gournay: Her Life and Works*. The Hague: Mouton, 1963.

Lodge, R. C. *Plato's Theory of Ethics: The Moral Criterion and the Highest Good*. London: Kegan Paul; New York: Harcourt, 1928.

Maclean, Ian. *Woman Triumphant: Feminism in French Literature 1610–1652*. Oxford: Clarendon Press, 1977.

McKinley, Mary. "An Editorial Revival: Gournay's 1617 Preface to the *Essais*." *Montaigne Studies: An Interdisciplinary Forum* 8.1–2 (1996): 193–201.

The Oxford Dictionary of English Proverbs. Comp. William George Smith. 3rd ed., rev. F. P. Wilson. Oxford: Clarendon Press, 1970.

Rigolot, François. Introduction. In "Préface à l'édition des *Essais* de Montaigne (Paris: Abel L'Angelier, 1595)," by Marie de Gournay, ed. François Rigolot, 8–20. *Montaigne Studies: An Interdisciplinary Forum* 1 (1989).

Sankovitch, Tilde A. *French Women Writers and the Book: Myths of Access and Desire.* Syracuse, NY: Syracuse University Press, 1988.

Sayce, Richard A., and David Maskell. *A Descriptive Bibliography of Montaigne's Essais, 1580–1700.* London: The Bibliographical Society and The Modern Humanities Research Association, 1983.

Schiff, Mario. *La fille d'alliance de Montaigne, Marie de Gournay.* 1910; repr. Geneva: Slatkine, 1978.

Shakespeare, William. *Hamlet. The Riverside Shakespeare.* Gen. eds. G. Blakemore Evans and J. J. M. Tobin. 2nd ed. Boston: Houghton Mifflin, 1997.

Stanton, Domna C. "Woman as Object and Subject of Exchange: Marie de Gournay's *Le Proumenoir* (1594)." *L'Esprit créateur* 23.2 (1983): 9–25.

Tetel, Marcel, ed. *Montaigne and Marie de Gournay. Journal of Medieval and Renaissance Studies* 25 (1995). (Special issue based on International Colloquium, Duke University, 31 March–1 April 1995.)

Venesoen, Constant. *Études sur la littérature féminine au XVIIe siècle: Mademoiselle de Gournay, Mademoiselle de Scudéry, Madame de Villedieu, Madame de Lafayette.* Birmingham, AL: Summa, 1990.

———. Introduction. In *Égalité des hommes et des femmes, Grief des dames, Le Proumenoir de Monsieur de Montaigne,* by Marie de Gournay, ed. Constant Venesoen, 7–15. Textes Littéraires Français. Geneva: Droz, 1993.

Villey, Pierre. *Montaigne devant la postérité.* Paris: Ancienne Librairie Furne, Boivin, [1935].

Yates, Frances A. *John Florio: The Life of an Italian in Shakespeare's England.* 1934; repr. New York: Octagon, 1968.

MRTS

MEDIEVAL & RENAISSANCE TEXTS & STUDIES
is the major publishing program of the
Arizona Center for Medieval and Renaissance Studies
at Arizona State University, Tempe, Arizona.

MRTS emphasizes books that are needed —
texts, translations, and major research tools.

MRTS aims to publish the highest quality scholarship
in attractive and durable format at modest cost.